S0-BCJ-393

"THE GREAT STORY"

21ST CENTURY CHRISTIAN
PUBLICATIONS

2809 Granny White Pike
Nashville, Tennessee 37204

"THE GREAT STORY"

TO BARBARA
who continues to inspire me
to preach God's Word.

Contents

Foreword

Genesis—the very word means "beginning," "roots," "origins." As we search for our "beginnings," we are led back to *Genesis*. *Genesis* is first, primary, crucial, necessary, central. *Genesis* is not about the periphery, but is right on target. Why *Genesis*? It is "The Great Story"; and because we all love stories, we love to read *Genesis*. It is not just any story, however. It is really the one story that makes sense to all of us. It is the one story that we all give attention to, that we all care about, and that we all need to hold on to in a changing world. It is the story of God and His relationship with mankind. Enjoy *Genesis*. It is a book of emotion, history, adventure, and mystery. It does not answer all of our questions, but it does answer our most important questions, our most human questions, our most necessary questions. *Genesis* is like a fascinating journey. The adventure is not only in the destination but in the trip itself. Like a mirror, *Genesis* reflects ourselves throughout its pages. We see our own lives in Abraham, Rebekah, Joseph, and many others. Life will become brighter and more attractive throughout our study of *Genesis*. Why? Because above all else in *Genesis*, we will meet God.

Dr. Prentice A. Meador, Jr.
Pulpit Minister
Prestoncrest church of Christ
Dallas, Texas

"The Great Story" (An Overview)

Henry Ward Beecher, in one of his Yale lectures on preaching, defines preaching in the following way: "Preaching is the art of moving men from a lower to a higher life. It is the art of inspiring them to a nobler manhood." A few years later, Phillips Brooks goes to that same university and delivers his lectures on preaching. He says that, "Preaching is the communication of truth by man to men. It has in it two essential elements, truth and personality. Neither of those can it spare and it still be preaching."

But what is God's way of communicating truth? How does God communicate to us? The truths that He wants to reveal to you and me—how does He put them into language? Are you not glad that He did not do it simply by philosophy or by myth? If it is not by myth or by philosophy, how does God communicate truths to us? It is by story.

COMMUNICATION BY STORY

Why is it that God communicates by story? With all of the options open to the most powerful, the greatest, the wisest, the most brilliant . . . with every possibility laid out before Him as to how He could communicate, why does He do it with a simple story?

First, we all love stories. Children love to hear a story before they go to bed. Why? A story makes children of us all. We all love stories.

Second, we remember a story. We do not forget it. There is something about a story that gets in the memory. Perhaps it is the process of identification. Perhaps it is the specifics that relate to our own lives. After all, we live a story and so stories are important to us. We do not forget a story.

Third, the story has a point. We participate in the story. So when God wants to communicate with you and me in His Word, He does not give us myth or philosophy. He gives us a story, and by reading that story we walk away from it saying, "That's me. I've done that. I've thought that. I have felt that. The very thing I see that's going on right here in the story is something that I participate in as I listen to the story." Soren Kierkegaard says, *"The gospel is not just a piece of information."* It is not just facts. It is a story that grabs your heart. It is a story that has passion and intensity and great relevance to our lives.

"THE GREAT STORY"

Genesis is "the great story." There are variations on it, but we will just dwell on "the great story." In Genesis 1, 2, and 3, "the great story" begins. In the beginning, God took nothing and made everything. He made the heavens, the stars, and the planets. He made the solar system and created life.

He creates the light containers—the sun, the moon, the stars. He then creates the noblest of all of His creations—mankind. There is celebration, joy, peace, wonder, and love. The relationship that the man and woman each have with God gives them an understanding of who they are, a meaning and purpose to their lives. There is a tremendous excitement about this. There is an enormous joy about it. There are no hospitals, no nursing homes, no homes for the aged, and no care centers. There are no confessions, no apologies, no mistakes, no misunderstandings, no confrontations, and no silences. There is joy, celebration, peace, and love. The point of "the great story" is that human life has meaning when it is connected with God. Human life has tremendous meaning and great purpose when life is related to God (Genesis 1—2).

HUMAN QUESTIONS ABOUT "THE GREAT STORY"

People have read Genesis 1 and 2 and have raised lots of questions about the story. Is this a myth, or is this literal? How long are the days in the days of creation? How do we measure time? We measure from a sunrise to a sunset. A day has twenty-four hours in it because we have a sunrise and a sunset. But when was the sun created? It was not created on the first day. Human beings raise the question about how long the days are. Humans give their own answers. The days must be twenty-four hours because our days are twenty-four hours. What happens on each of those days? Humans raise questions about how did it happen, and when did it happen? Men raise the questions regarding science and the creation account. In the last twenty or twenty-five years, man has theorized that everything started with the "Big Bang" theory. This amounts to the latest human explanation regarding Genesis.

Each question is a human question; it is not a God question. God never raises the question of myth versus literal, nor length of days, nor how everything came into being. These questions are not raised by God, but by humans. *These human questions, while interesting to man's curiosity, greatly distract from "the great story."* Why do humans raise such questions? There may be several reasons, but such questions tend to move the mind of man away from the major point of "the great story." "The great story" has one point: *Human life only has meaning when connected to God.*

FAITH ACCEPTS "THE GREAT STORY"

Distracting questions miss the whole point of "the great story." No human being is there when the events of Genesis 1—3 take place. To accept these events is to believe the story by faith. Our own defense is what our faith does for our personal lives. If you disbelieve "the great story," that is your faith. And you must ask, "What has *not* believing in 'the great story' done for my life?" Does it bring you peace, purpose, meaning, hope, and does it allow you to face death? I like what faith does for the lives of some people I know who believe "the great story." It brings peace when nothing else will. It allows people to look right into the eyes of death and laugh at it and not be frightened. It causes people to realize that something is bigger than science, chemistry, physics, geology, and history. That something is *God.* That may not be your faith, but then I would have to ask you the question, "What has *not believing* in the basic story done for your life?"

> Now faith is the assurance of things hoped for, the conviction of things not seen. For by it the men of old gained approval. By faith we understand that the worlds were prepared by the word of God, so that what is seen was not made out of things which are visible (Hebrews 11:1-3).

The Bible puts it on the basis of faith. That is what the story calls for in each of us.

THE REST OF THE STORY

Something now happens in "the great story." Genesis 3 tells of guilt, shame, hiding, breakdown, hatred, and self-consciousness. Cain then kills Abel. God asks, "Where is your brother?" Man responds, "Am I my brother's keeper?" When you live in relationship with God, you love your brother. That is what life is all about. That is what "the great story" is trying to teach us. When God is your source of relationship, there will not be family breakup, war, political struggle, and violence. In the midst of the breakdown, spiritual death occurs. What is the response of God?

"THE GREAT STORY"— GOD'S RESPONSE

Genesis 6 gives God's response as He floods the earth, establishes a loving covenant with man, and calls man to walk with Him again. It is a call of "Let's go back to the Garden of Eden. Let's do this again. I love you." Remember the point of "the great story": *Human life has meaning when it is connected to God.* Man breaks the relationship with God, yet the love of God and the call of God come again. The rest of Genesis is understood in the context of that story. The rest of the Bible is simply a version of that story. The life of Jesus Christ and the gospel of Jesus Christ is the presentation of that story again. God wants to walk with you and me. He wants to go back to that relationship He once had with us. Jesus comes and says, "I am God." These are God's words. These are God's actions. "I'm laying down My life so you can live with Me. Life only has meaning when it is connected to God." "The great story" continues by calling upon every person to do this: "Repent, and let each of you be baptized in the name of Jesus Christ for the forgiveness of your sins; and you shall receive the gift of the Holy Spirit." Human life only has meaning if it is connected to God, the Father.

CLUES IN "THE GREAT STORY"

The story gives us some clues as to what God is really up to. The story gives us eyes to see and ears to hear the Bible. Do you see why men and women who are very aged and have been Christians for many years go back and keep studying Genesis? It is "the great story." It is the basic story about which the rest of the whole Bible develops.

What does "the great story" teach us?
1. It tells us what we need to know about God.
2. It tells us how to be right with God.
3. It gives us our best understanding of ourselves.
4. It gives us a rationale for living life.
5. It provides us with a framework within which to deal with our struggles, problems, and failures.
6. It gives us hope and strengthens our faith.

The following are three practical suggestions for preaching on Genesis:
1. Spend crucial time in Genesis.
2. Do not miss the point of "the great story."
3. Delight that God calls for faith to accept "the great story."

CONCLUSION

He wants you to be in concert with Him. He wants to be in harmony with you. He wants balance between you and Him. That is why He has brought us Genesis. Jesus comes and says, in effect, "I am the Word. In the beginning I was there. . . . All things were made through Me" (John 1:1-3).

One person was there. That is Jesus, the Christ. He was there, and everything was made through Him. We can put our faith in Him.

QUESTIONS

1. Why does God communicate by "story"?

2. Why is Genesis so open to human questions which tend to distract from "the great story"?

3. What is the point of "the great story"?

4. What are some of the clues as to what God is really up to in "the great story"?

5. What suggestions would you add to the three given in this chapter on preaching on Genesis?

Caution:
God at Work

Open ditches, mounds of dirt, bulldozers, earth movers, cement trucks—whenever you see these you usually see blinking yellow lights and a sign reading: "Caution: Men at Work." In a similar way, there are moments in Scripture that call our attention to God at work. They just stand out. They grab your attention like those yellow blinking caution lights. They say, "Slow up at this point." Such Scriptures signify: "Caution: God at Work!" Significant questions develop around these caution points: What is God's purpose? What significance does it have for us as human beings? How does God connect to human life? What does this Scripture mean to my life?

The Scripture presents two major moments when God really is at work. Of course, He is at work every day since He gives you bread and brings you water. He answers your prayer. He is at work all of the time. Scripture points to the work of God in magnificent and unusual ways.

In the New Testament, Scripture draws special attention to the cross of Jesus Christ. It is like one of those yellow blinking lights in Scripture. It stops you and tells you God is at work right here in the death, the burial, and the resurrection of Jesus Christ.

In the Old Testament, there is another special, magnificent moment. Those yellow blinking lights in Scripture begin to flash and draw your attention to the work of God. It is the creation by God. It is found in the great book of Genesis.

GENESIS—THE KEY TO THE BIBLE

Genesis is the key to the whole Bible. This is actually not an overstatement. You must understand Genesis 1—3 to understand Genesis 4—12. You must understand Genesis 4—12 to understand Genesis 13—36. You must understand Genesis 13—36 to understand Genesis 37—50. Here is the key: You must understand Genesis to understand the rest of the Bible. Why is Genesis the key to the Bible? Because if you do not understand Genesis, you do not know the origin of Israel. If you do not know the origin of Israel, you do not have the slightest idea what is happening in the Old Testament or in much of the New Testament. Without an understanding of the origin of Israel, how do you make any sense of the ministry of Jesus? If you do not know the origin of Israel, how do you understand the beginning of the church in Acts? If you do not know the origin of Israel, how do you understand the epistles of the New Testament? Genesis is the key that unlocks the entire Word of God. Everything begins in Genesis.

GENESIS SPEAKS TO DEEP HUMAN CONCERNS

My friend Landon Saunders and I were visiting Brazil for the 1988 Pan American Lectureships. In one of his presentations, he listed the concerns of people today. He could have taken those concerns from today's media, newspapers, and news magazines. He is right on target, however, in developing those needs from Genesis.

In a similar way, let us list some of the concerns that human beings have today: violence (war and crime); marriage and family; labor and management; relationships between man and woman; death; afterlife and eternity; guilt, meaninglessness, and purposelessness; low self-esteem and depression; and environment.

Genesis gives the story of how God meets each of the above needs and concerns. Genesis gives not only the first answer of God to these questions but the final answer to each of these issues. In a world that searches for more and more technology to solve human questions, the real answers are given in Genesis.

All of the Bible is about Genesis. The Bible is not about something else. It is about what is in Genesis, and it is only about what is in Genesis. The aims and purposes of God are revealed in Genesis. The relationships we are to have as human beings are revealed in Genesis. The plan of God is laid down in Genesis. The rest of the Bible is but a development of "the great story" that is found in Genesis. Even though the story depicts different events and persons in the rest of the Bible, "the great story" remains the same. So Genesis is the key to understanding the Bible.

If Genesis is the key and it addresses our basic concerns as human beings, how does it do it? Genesis presents what I call "the great story." We are living in the twentieth century, living this side of Charles Darwin, in a time in which our young people are taught the scientific method and the ability to distinguish knowledge that is scientifically determined as opposed to any other way. Due to the heavy scientific and technological emphasis of our time, it is important to understand what Genesis is about and what it is *not* about. Genesis is not about certain things. We have to clear some ground so we can plant some seed.

1. Genesis is not about the controversy between evolution and creation.
2. Genesis is not about science and technology.

3. Genesis is not about religion.

4. Genesis is not about philosophy.

These disclaimers are necessary because as we approach Genesis 1:1 many of us are wearing glasses, and those glasses are fogged by philosophy, evolution, science, and religion. Genesis is not about any of that. Let us illustrate how our own self-imposed glasses keep us from the real point of Genesis.

Many people, when they read Genesis 1:1, ask, "Are these really twenty-four-hour days? That's what I'm really interested in. What I want to know is how scientifically valid is this story anyway? What is the date of the first day? How does everything come into being?" When people read Genesis asking Genesis to answer their own human questions, they look at the text through their own self-imposed glasses. All of this distracts us from the point of "the great story" ... that this is God! God has taken action. Furthermore, we can know all of the facts about Genesis 1 and 2 and never know God. But Genesis 1 and 2 is not written to cause us just to be able to recite facts, nor is it just a piece of information. We can know all of the facts and miss the joy, the mystery, and the life of Genesis 1 and 2.

THE THEME OF GENESIS

What is it about? Genesis is about God and what God is up to. We have no speech to really talk about God outside of the Bible. All we have to use in order to talk about God are symbols. You have to be careful when you are talking about God that you use the symbols that God has given you, not symbols that some philosopher, scientist, preacher, or someone else has given you. For example, many of us learned what is called the big Omni about God. God is omnipresent, omniscient, and omnipotent—the big three. Aristotle gave us those. But what I am saying is that did not come from Moses. It did not come from David. You ask, What is the problem with that? If you take everything you know about God and put it in one of those three categories, you immediately have gotten off the subject of Genesis. You have been distracted from what Genesis is trying to say to you. You have taken a human being's three categories, and you have put the living God in them. The Bible does not do that. Greek philosophy does. But the Word of God never puts God in three neat pigeonholes. Why? He will not fit. You just cannot get Him in there. Those three labels are not going to describe the God of Genesis. So be careful with the language you use to describe God.

The God of Genesis is a God who speaks, and when He speaks it is like nothing human beings have ever heard. The God of Genesis can be so silent that you wonder if He will ever speak again. The God of Genesis is a God who reveals Himself, and when you look at Him you are just awestruck. You just go to your knees and worship Him when He reveals Himself. His power, His purpose, His beauty, His holiness, and His immense love cause you to drop to your knees when He reveals Himself. But He can conceal Himself so that you wonder if you ever saw Him in the first place. He is a God of mystery. He is a God you will never categorize. He is a God you will never understand. He is beyond the intellect of any human being. It is, therefore, to be understood that He is mysterious. He speaks, and He is silent. He is here, but He is there. He is silent, and He reveals. He conceals and pulls back, and He intrudes and shows who He is. In our day and time and our way of looking at life—rationalism—secular humanism—it causes us to miss the real point of "the great story."

"The great story" is great because it touches the greatest depths in the human spirit every time you tell it. That is why children love to hear it. It is the most important story that man has ever heard. It is new and fresh every time you tell it. So let us briefly tell it.

AN OVERVIEW OF "THE GREAT STORY"

> In the beginning God created the heavens and the earth (1:1).

Dr. Arthur Compton, Nobel Prize winner in physics in 1923, states his faith in the *Chicago Daily News*, April 12, 1936:

> For myself, faith begins with a realization that a supreme intelligence brought the universe into being and created man. It is not difficult for me to have this faith, for it is incontrovertible that where there is a plan there is intelligence—an orderly, unfolding universe testifies to the truth of the most majestic statement ever uttered—"In the beginning God."

In this indefinite period of time, there existed God. We have no way of knowing the length of time of the beginning.

> And the earth was formless and void, . . . (1:2).

No human being knows how long this condition existed. This could have taken billions or trillions of years. Only God knows. I was not there. You were not there. You have never met or read of anybody who was there. Only God was there in the beginning when He created the heavens and the earth. How He did it is His mystery.

Read Genesis 1:3-25. God creates night and day, divides the waters, and creates earth and seas. He produces vegetation. Then He creates sun, moon, and stars. You can see from the text what pleasure God receives from His creation. God is at work, and this is joyful. "And God saw that it was good." Having created living plants and creatures to produce "after their kind," we see the vast biological system of God's handiwork: species, genus, family, order, class, and phylum.

> "Let Us make man in Our image, . . ." (1:26, 27).

Then God came to His greatest creation. He created mankind like Himself. The words "create," "make," and "form" are applied to the activity of God toward mankind. From nothing, God builds mankind with a spirit like Himself. "Let Us" refers to the Trinity present at creation and reminds us of John 1:1-3, where Christ is not only present at creation, but actively participates in it with God and the Holy Spirit. Note also that God created mankind into sexual beings prior to any other relationships. In a world confused over the whole subject of "sex," it is crucial to see that God created "male and female" before the fall of mankind. He considers sexuality to be "good" along with all of the creation of God. He said let them rule over all of this, the fish, the birds, the livestock, the earth, and the creatures. He told them to be fruitful and multiply and rule over the earth and subdue the earth.

> And God saw all that He had made, and behold, it was very good. And there was evening and there was morning, the sixth day (1:31).

Do you catch the theme that is running through this about God? Here is the story of God's deep joy. He creates birds, animals, and mankind all in a moment of joy. Here is the story of human life. Have you wondered more about anything than our origin? We are not mere accidents. We came out of a special moment of the joy of God. God created every man, woman, boy, and girl in His own spirit.

A STORY OF RELATIONSHIPS

Genesis 2:1-25 is a zoom lens effect of chapter 1.

Chapter 1 is the story of origins. Chapter 2 is the story of relationships. The first relationship tells us about God and mankind. There is joy, closeness, and oneness. There is freedom, clarity, and celebration. There is love, balance, and harmony. There is communication, understanding, and unity. This is the way God wants it between Himself and His greatest of all creations, man and woman.

There is the story of the second relationship. It is the account of mankind and the planet. God places mankind over his environment and directs mankind "to cultivate it and keep it." He gives him instructions on how to do it. He has already told man and woman in His blessing, "rule over the fish of the sea and over the birds of the sky, and over every living thing that moves on the earth." Man and woman are masters, not servants, of planet Earth. Man and woman live within boundaries just like the boundaries that God has fixed for all of His creation. The boundaries give shape, order, and harmony. Mankind nurtures, cares, and protects all of God's earth. It is a sacred trust.

The third relationship is man and woman, or really, husband and wife. You read the moment of joy in the creation of woman as you read 2:23:

> And the man said, "This is now bone of my bones, and flesh of my flesh; she shall be called Woman, because she was taken out of Man."

The English word "this" just does not do the Hebrew word justice at all. We translate it "this" because we do not have a good word. If I were to give it my translation of the Hebrew, it would read that when Adam first saw Eve, when the husband saw his wife for the very first time, having looked at all the other creation God has given, he then said, "Ah! Hah!" There is real joy. If you are Adam, how do you communicate with a star? How does a fish listen to a human being? God saw that it was not good for man to be alone. So He made him someone like himself. "Ah! Hah!" The joy of man and woman, of husband and wife. "This is now bone of my bones, and flesh of my flesh." This is different from birds and fish and planets and stars.

> For this cause a man shall leave his father and his mother, and shall cleave to his wife; and they shall

become one flesh. And the man and his wife were both naked and were not ashamed (2:24, 25).

The relationship was not full of shame. Instead, the relationship was caring, oneness, unity, closeness, permanence, pleasure, and laughter. It was unique and special. There was touching and enjoyment, worth and value, importance and self-esteem.

THE SIGNIFICANCE OF "THE GREAT STORY"

What is the power of "the great story"? Let me give five truths about it.

1. It teaches us about our key relationships.
2. It causes us to worship God and not self. It causes us to wonder. It lifts our eyes above planet Earth to the heavens and to God.
3. It raises great questions, answers some, and solves the basic concerns of human beings.
4. It helps us to understand the rest of the Bible.
5. It may be told with freshness and newness every time.

"The great story" is a story we believe by faith because the only one who was there was God. "In the beginning was the Word, and the Word was with God, and the Word was God. . . . All things came into being by Him, and apart from Him nothing came into being that has come into being" (John 1:1, 3). We believe by faith. Some may listen to "the great story" and not believe it. Let me recite two sentences of two great skeptics who did not believe Genesis 1 and 2.

First, the French philosopher Voltaire said, "I tremble to have complained once more of this being of beings. In casting an attentive eye over this terrible picture, I wish I had never been born. . . ."[1]

Robert Ingersol, known as "The Great Agnostic,"

---

[1] John Cairns, *Unbelief in the Eighteenth Century* (Edinburgh, Scotland: Adam & Charles Black, 1881), 141.

said, "Life is a narrow vale between the cold and barren peaks of two eternities. We strive in vain to look beyond the heights, we cry aloud and the only answer is the echo of our wailing cry."[2]

Contrast the results and the consequences of skepticism with the consequences of faith. After a life of faith Paul says, ". . . I know whom I have believed and I am convinced that He is able to guard what I have entrusted to Him until that day" (2 Timothy 1:12). Just before his death, Paul affirms his faith by saying, "I can do all things through Him who strengthens me" (Philippians 4:13).

QUESTIONS

1. Is it an overstatement that "Genesis is the key that unlocks the entire word of God"? Why?

2. What human concerns are mentioned in Genesis and how does "the great story" focus upon them?

3. What is Genesis not about?

4. What is the theme of Genesis?

5. Why is "the great story" so significant?

---

[2]A. Craig Baird, *American Public Address 1740-1942* (New York: McGraw Hill, 1956), 179.

3   Genesis 3—5

Paradise Lost

"Genesis is not an independent book that can be interpreted by itself," claims Gerhard von Rad.[1] There can be no doubt that Genesis is the key to everything. Two examples illustrate the great significance of Genesis to the rest of the Bible. For instance, the speech of Joshua before Israel at Shechem (Joshua 24:2-13) gives the basic review of the history of Israel as found in Genesis. Second, when Stephen gives an outline of the history of Israel, he depends heavily upon Genesis. If one is to really understand what is going on in all of the Old Testament, one must understand Genesis. It is equally true that if one is to understand what is going on in the New Testament, particularly in the ministry of Jesus Christ and the beginning of the church, one has to understand Genesis.

The format of Genesis is "the great story." God knows that we remember stories, so He tells Genesis in a story form. In Genesis 1 and 2 God crowns His creation with His most noble effort—the creation of mankind. God gives mankind their freedom of choice. With freedom came joy. Man and woman and God live in

---

[1]Gerhard von Rad, *Genesis*, trans. John H. Marks (London: SCM Press, 1961), 13.

balance. Their relationship is one that is extremely beautiful, and it is one in which they give to one another out of their communication to each other. There is no regret, no guilt. There is no problem, no tears. There are no nursing homes, hospitals, or orphanages. The relationship between mankind and God is one with closeness and harmony.

THE BROKEN RELATIONSHIP (3)

> Now the serpent was more crafty than any beast
> of the field which the Lord God had made.... (3:1).

It is at this point that something begins to interfere in the relationship. The relationship between God and mankind is what Genesis is all about. That is what the Bible is about. That is what Christ is about. That is what the church is about. Genesis is about relationships between God and mankind and man and man. To fail to see this is to fail to understand what is about to happen. What is about to happen is a breaking of the relationships.

The tempter comes in a disguise. Notice that he is not coming to man and woman in a red suit with a pitchfork calling attention to himself. Rather, evil comes dressed in religious concern—wanting to talk about ultimate things, like God and who God is. Satan does not come to mankind as an atheistic monster who says, "I'm going to destroy your paradise today.... God is an illusion. . . . He really doesn't exist!" Rather, Satan comes and says, "Today I want to talk to you about God." This, of course, inspires confidence in any human being and reveals that the tempter believes in God. He plans his strategy with piety and with Scripture. He looks holy, reverent, concerned, and devout. He begins his seductions.

The seduction takes place in part because mankind does not recognize the tempter as the tempter. What we have here is what one scholar calls a "religious devil," but I would submit to you that he is always religious. His deepest concern is about religion, God, man, and our relationship to God. And so, the discussion begins between man, woman, and the tempter.

> ... And he said to the woman, "Indeed, has God said, 'You shall not eat from any tree of the garden'?" (3:1).

The question hits Eve at a vulnerable place. He sows two poisonous seeds into the man and the woman. The first one is this: "God is really different from the way that you think of God. It is okay to believe in Him. It is all right to give Him something, but hold back something for yourself. It is even all right to give Him the center and just keep the periphery." Eve's answer begins to show that she has, in a very real way, accepted the planting of this poisonous seed that God is really very different from the way she perceives Him.

> ... "You surely shall not die! For God knows that in the day you eat from it your eyes will be opened, and you will be like God, knowing good and evil" (3:4, 5).

This is a second poisonous seed: "You really should not trust the goodness of God." When Satan tells her, "You will not die," he means, of course, "God would not do that to you." He sows doubt about the goodness of God in her heart. If God would do that, then God would not be good. If Satan can ever wedge into the human heart that God may not be good, if I ever believe that God is not good, then I am vulnerable to other things about God—He may not love me; He may not care for me; He may not even exist as God. You can run your own affairs. You will be like God. You will know good from evil just like God knows good from evil. After all, God knows that if you eat of this fruit you will be like Him, and He does not want you to be like Him.

When the woman saw that the tree was good for

food, and that it was a delight to the eyes, and that
the tree was desirable to make one wise, she took
from its fruit and ate; . . . (3:6).

Then the tempter appeals to her through three basic
avenues of tempation. "When the woman saw that the
tree was good for food" (when it appealed to her flesh),
then, when the woman saw "that it was a delight to the
eyes" (here is the desire of the lust of the eye), and third,
she saw "that the tree was desirable to make one wise"
(here is pride). Those are the three basic avenues Satan
always uses to approach mankind. The New Testament will call it the lust of the flesh, the lust of the eyes,
and the boastful pride of life (1 John 2:16). Each of these
avenues makes its way into the very basic nature of
mankind.

With the decision to disobey God, Adam and Eve
exercise their free choice. God did not program us like a
computer. God did not make us like puppets and pull
little strings in order to make us obey Him. God created
us and gave us freedom of choice and then said, in
effect, "You must choose whether you will obey Me or
disobey Me." What a marvelous expression of love. It is
a gift of being created in the image of God. This is what
it is like to be spiritual. It means we have freedom. But
with freedom always comes responsibility. And, what
the woman is about to do is exercise her freedom of
choice, and then she will begin to bring down serious
consequences of her action. "She took from its fruit and
ate."

But you know what happens to Eve when she dis-
obeys God? Whenever we exercise our freedom of choice
and we choose to disobey God, we then die. She starts
dying spiritually. She has placed herself in a situation
in which she is now going to be apart from God. She
made that choice. As she exercises the choice, now
comes the first major consequence, she will now spiritually die. She will spiritually be separated from God.

". . . and she gave also to her husband with her, and he ate" (3:6). Then, they become self-conscious. They become aware of evil in themselves. Now, they feel guilt. Sin damages our self-esteem and our appreciation of others. It severs our relationships with God and man. Our knowledge of evil causes us, like Adam and Eve, to feel "naked" in the presence of a loving Father.

The Lord then comes walking through the garden, and He asks the first question in the Old Testament, "Where are you?" (The first question in the New Testament is, "Where is He who has been born King of the Jews?") He is not asking a question of location. He is asking, "Where is the relationship we once had? We were close. We loved each other. We walked in balance. I loved you. You loved Me. We walked together. What has happened to the relationship?" And the man answered, "I heard the sound of Thee in the garden, and I was afraid because I was naked; so I hid myself." That is a rational answer. It is a man's answer. It is a humanistic answer. It is a good answer, if you are a human being. "I hid because I was naked," reasons man. But God confronts Adam, "There is just one problem—who told you you were naked? How did you become aware of your condition? When did you start hiding from Me? When did you start feeling guilt? When did you start feeling bad about yourself? When did you start feeling low self-esteem? When did you start putting yourself down? Who told you that you were naked?" The man then immediately blames: "The woman whom Thou gavest to be with me, she gave me from the tree, and I ate." The woman blames the serpent. Then, of course, the rest of the chapter is the curse. God condemns the serpent, the woman, and the man to experience the results of their actions.

Do you realize what the story is telling us about ourselves? We have the freedom to make our own choices, to choose our own thoughts, to choose our own eternity. We choose our relationships. We choose how we will feel about ourselves. We choose how we will handle responsibility. We make these choices—profound choices. Choices have ultimate consequences. The story says, "So He drove the man out; and at the east of the garden of Eden He stationed the cherubim, and the flaming sword which turned every direction, to guard the way to the tree of life" (3:24). The relationship is broken. The "oneness" between God and mankind is severed. The relationship horizontally is now broken.

THE BREAKING OF RELATIONSHIPS (4)

In the course of time Cain and Abel both bring offerings before the Lord God. Cain brings some of the fruits of the soil. Abel brings some of the fat portions of the firstborn of the Lord. The Lord has told them what to bring. Abel does it. His brother does not. And so the Lord looks with great favor upon Abel and upon his offering: "By faith Abel offered to God a better sacrifice than Cain, through which he obtained the testimony that he was righteous, God testifying about his gifts, . . ." (Hebrews 11:4). Cain begins to feel jealousy and envy in his own heart. He decides to break the relationship with his own brother. ". . . Cain rose up against Abel his brother and killed him" (4:8), but Cain's attack begins with his uncontrolled anger. ". . . So Cain became very angry and his countenance fell" (4:5). The Hebrew word translated "angry" means "burn." Cain apparently feels deep resentment and a deep-seated hostility which results in depression and the murder of Abel.

> Then the Lord said to Cain, "Why are you angry? And why has your countenance fallen? If you do well, will not your countenance be lifted up? And if you do not do well, sin is crouching at the door; and its desire is for you, but you must master it" (4:6, 7).

God seems to be telling Cain, "I will restore you to a place of fellowship with Me. I'll lift depression from you. But you must do what is right. If you decide to not do right, sin is like an animal lying in wait at your door, and it will destroy you if you do not master it." The point of the text is simple and clear; mankind was created to be mastered by God, or else mankind will be the slave of sin through his own passions and desires. To be a slave of God means eternal life. To be a slave of sin means eternal death. Cain makes his choice and slaughters his brother.

When the relationship between man and God is broken, every other relationship in life horizontally is severed. The marriage relationship breaks. The family relationship breaks. The friendship relationship breaks. The community relationship breaks. It is all torn apart. And, as one scholar has said, "When mankind decided to unite in sin we became disunited in everything else." It is now in pieces at the foot of the Creator. All the relationships that He built are now in pieces.

> Then the Lord said to Cain, "Where is Abel your brother?" And he said, "I do not know. Am I my brother's keeper?" (4:9).

There is no sense of remorse over the horrible violence against Abel. So paramount is this violence that John will caution Christians to remember the example of Cain: "Not as Cain, who was of the evil one, and slew his brother. And for what reason did he slay him? Because his deeds were evil, and his brother's were righteous. . . . Everyone who hates his brother is a murderer; and you know that no murderer has eternal life abiding in him" (1 John 3:12, 15). The heart of Cain becomes so calloused that there is no sense of repentance. He asks the question that mankind has been asking ever since: "Am I my brother's keeper?"

We have established universities to answer that question. We have sponsored all kinds of research to find an answer to that question. We have looked up and down history for an answer to that question. Do I have any responsibility to another human being? That question still haunts the human race. "Am I my brother's keeper?" We still quote it in speeches. Poets still write about it. Movie makers still make films about it. Here is the question that lies at the very heart and at the very center of all of the human relationship problems. You do not get any deeper than this. Am I responsible for my behavior toward other human beings? When Jesus came to this world, He gave an answer to this question. Apparently it is so easy for religious people to misunderstand the ministry of Jesus. The religious people of His day and time looked at it and never could quite see that when He was helping this leper, feeding this hungry woman, taking care of this bruised person . . . that was the soul of one of them lying there. Jesus picked up their souls, and He loved them by laying down His soul beside theirs. And the ministry of Jesus answers the question. Jesus says that is what our religion is all about. That is what Genesis is all about. First, it is about your relationship to God. Because you are your brother's keeper, Genesis is also about your relationship to your fellow man.

We in the church, therefore, must love each other. We must never do what Cain did. We must never hurt each other. Why is He saying that? Because that is what it is all about. We become Christians to be each other's keeper. Why do we minister to those in prison? Why do we go to the streets and feed the hungry? Why does the youth minister have a retreat and minister to the inner city? Why do we come together to worship God? Why do people place their membership in our churches? What is this religion all about? It is about the story. It is about loving God first, and then loving your neighbor as you love yourself.

The story takes us to the time in which human beings come to this earth and begin to populate it, and the relationships are torn and shattered and lie in pieces at the foot of the Creator. One writer I read in preparation for this special Genesis series said that Genesis 3 is the saddest chapter in the Bible. It may well be.

HEALING THE RELATIONSHIPS

Jesus Christ comes along hundreds of years later and makes a profound statement when He says: "I am the way, and the truth, and the life; no one comes to the Father, but through Me" (John 14:6). *Now* there is a way. *Now* there is truth. *Now* there is life. *Now* there is a way to get back to Him. *Now* there is a way of relationship again with Him. *Now* there is a way for me to learn that I am my brother's keeper. When I make choices, those choices impact on my fellow men. The relationships can be restored through Christ. But, here is the kicker! As we made a choice to *break* them, we must make a choice to *make* them. Now the choice is ours to make a relationship with Him. Is that not beautiful? Is that not powerful? Is that not tremendous? Does that not tug at your spirit, your heart, and your emotions? You do not have to eternally be spiritually separated from God. Here is the grace, the majesty, and the love of God. He gives it in Christ to bring us back to Him and to each other. Stay in Him. Die in Him because you have life that He has given you.

QUESTIONS

1. What does it mean that Genesis is about "relationships"?

2. What relationships were broken when mankind lost Paradise?

3. What are the two poisonous seeds which the tempter sows into man and woman?

4. What does "the great story" tell us about choices?

5. Why is the relationship between man and God primary?

The Flood

A WORLD WITHOUT GOD

If there had been any newspapers and television news reports, they would have carried frightening statistics! Figures would have been released by governments to indicate the complete breakdown of family life, law, moral responsibility, and even conscience. There would have been reports of robberies taking place every two seconds, of an increase in violent crime, and of rape and murder taking place every two minutes. Stories would have been told of people living in fear. Though enlightened, even sophisticated, many citizens would have felt as though they were hostages living in their own countries. People would have gotten their kicks by terrorizing the elderly, frightening and raping women, and showing total disregard for human rights.

What had gone wrong? What had happened to the sophisticated world filled with language, accomplishment, achievement, and work? What had caused chaos and moral confusion? What had happened to the old rules? Were there no more standards, limits, or borders? Was nothing forbidden? Was civilization on the brink of destruction? Was the world out of control? The answer to all of these questions leads to Genesis 6.

GOD'S CREATION MISSES THE MARK
(6:1-12)

> Now it came about, when men began to multiply on the face of the land, and daughters were born to them, that the sons of God saw that the daughters of men were beautiful; and they took wives for themselves, whomever they chose (6:1, 2).

What is the problem described in the marriage of the "sons of God" with the "daughters of men"? Certainly it is not marriage which God ordained and created in the very beginning. The mosaic described in the early chapters of Genesis presents man as attempting to live independently of God. For example, Eve wants to be like God while Cain becomes angry at God's rejection, and later the people at Babel will try to become like God. These marriages were wrong because spiritual people were uniting themselves with earthly-minded people. Pride drives these marriages into the text so that we become aware of what man is becoming—a creature without God.

> Then the Lord said, "My Spirit shall not strive with man forever, because he also is flesh; nevertheless his days shall be one hundred and twenty years" (6:3).

The meaning of God's statement is debated by various scholars. The meaning would seem to be that God is saying that His Spirit will not remain in man forever because man is mortal. Something has happened in the relationship between God and man which is causing God to make certain decisions. God will not violate the free will of mankind. He will not force man to be good or virtuous. Compulsory love, faith, and hope is a contradiction in terms. Only man can decide to have faith, hope, and love, regardless of how much God wants this lifestyle for man. God is clearly reaching a point where He is so disturbed at the condition of man that a final decision is about to be made.

What does God mean when he says, "His days shall be one hundred and twenty years"? Some scholars believe that God has now decided to reduce to 120 years man's previously very long life span. This does not seem to be the correct interpretation since several of the patriarchs (Shem, Abraham, and Isaac) will live to be much older than 120. The passage would seem to mean that God is now allowing another 120 years for mankind to change before He destroys the earth by water. God's grace and love cause Him to show mercy.

> Then the Lord saw that the wickedness of man was great on the earth, and that every intent of the thoughts of his heart was only evil continually (6:5).

In the course of God's relationship to mankind, God is able to know the heart condition of His creation. Throughout the Word of God, man's deeds are the natural results of what is going on in his heart. The real question that God places constantly before people is the paramount question: "Who rules your heart?" At the very beginning, man decided that God would make His home in man's heart. Balance, order, purpose, meaning, joy, faithfulness, and love characterize that first relationship with God. By now, man has decided that he wants to live his life without God in his heart, and a moral vacuum takes place.

> And the Lord was sorry that He had made man on the earth, and He was grieved in His heart (6:6).

Sometimes the Scriptures are so blatantly clear, unreserved, and frank that it provides the reader with great difficulty. God is so deeply hurt at the intent and action of mankind that it gives Him grief. When mankind sins, God is sorry at the wickedness and evil of his actions. Before we humanize God and bring Him down to our level, we must remember that God is the Divine Spirit with attributes of holiness, justice, freedom, and love. His actions are not totally understood by mankind, and His will is often a mystery known to man only when God reveals it.

> And the Lord said, "I will blot out man whom I have created from the face of the land, from man to animals to creeping things and to birds of the sky; for I am sorry that I have made them" (6:7).

God decides that a universal and general destruction will now overtake all of mankind. Its story will be an eternal memory of God's divine wrath against man's sins. The pain of God is so immense that He feels grief for having created mankind.

> But Noah found favor in the eyes of the Lord. . . . Noah was a righteous man, blameless in his time;
> . . . (6:8-12).

Noah and his family are the only exceptions to God's decision to destroy all of mankind. At the very heart of God is everlasting love, mercy, and grace, and this passage reveals clearly the wonderful grace of God. Even though Noah is a man of virtue and goodness and even though he walks with God, the basis of his salvation from the flood rests in the grace of God.

THE FLOOD (6:13—7:24)

John Whitcomb and Henry Morris in their book entitled *The Genesis Flood* include the descriptions of the destructive power of modern-day floods. These descriptions detail how boulders of rock and granite up to two hundred tons in weight are easily moved by flood waters. The water cuts out deep gorges and turns cliffs into pebbles. Ordinary streams become raging oceans, and debris collects in astonishing amounts. The authors conclude that if this is the kind of destruction that can occur in a few hours or days, imagine the destruction of the biblical flood which hit the entire earth for forty days and forty nights.

> Then God said to Noah, "The end of all flesh has come before Me; for the earth is filled with violence because of them; . . . Make for yourself an ark. . . . And behold, I, even I am bringing the flood of water upon the earth, . . . And of every living thing of all flesh, you shall bring two of every kind into the ark, to keep them alive with you; they shall be male and female. . . ." Thus Noah did; according to all that God had commanded him, so he did (6:13-22).

Perhaps you have heard Bill Cosby's recording of God's conversation with Noah. Cosby's point demonstrates that human beings would probably think Noah should be committed to a mental institution. No doubt, most of mankind rejected Noah's counsel and preaching as he called upon them to repent and turn back to God. They thought, of course, that he was out of his mind to daily be building an ark. The ark is rectangular in shape and approximately 450 feet long, 75 feet wide, and 45 feet high. God's plan is for Noah to bring in every type of land animal into the ark and to store enough food for both the animals and Noah's family to eat. Noah obeys God in every detail.

> Then the Lord said to Noah, "Enter the ark, you and all your household; for you alone I have seen to be righteous before Me in this time. . . . For after seven more days, I will send rain on the earth forty days and forty nights; . . ." (7:1-24).

It is natural that Noah would obey God in all that God has commanded. Obedience is the natural result of being in a right relationship with God. Noah does not trust in himself or seek to elevate himself to the level of divinity. Instead, Noah relies upon God and fills his heart with God who rules his life. This accounts for God finding Noah to be "righteous before Me in this time."

The flood begins in the 600th year of Noah's life.
Noah and his family will leave the ark during the 601st
year of Noah's life. The flood begins by the great
underground rivers gushing water upward and the
great heavens above bringing down heavy rains. Many
nations record in their own history the presence of an
ancient flood which destroyed their civilization. The
flood is a major argument against the doctrine of
uniformitarianism—the view which maintains that
nature has never been interrupted. For instance, Peter
uses the flood for this very reason in 2 Peter 3:5-7:

> For when they maintain this, it escapes their
> notice that by the word of God the heavens existed
> long ago and the earth was formed out of water
> and by water, through which the world at that time
> was destroyed, being flooded with water. But the
> present heavens and earth by His word are being
> reserved for fire, kept for the day of judgment and
> destruction of ungodly men.

Peter uses the flood as his final argument for those who
choose to remain in willful rebellion against God and
who argue that nothing has ever changed since the
beginning. Peter also provides powerful New Testament support for the universality of the flood.

THE LAND OF BEGINNING AGAIN
(8:1—10:32)

> But God remembered Noah. . . . Then it came
> about at the end of forty days, that Noah opened
> the window of the ark which he had made; and he
> sent out a raven, . . . Then God spoke to Noah,
> saying, "Go out of the ark, you and your wife and
> your sons and your sons' wives with you. . . ." Then
> Noah built an altar to the Lord, . . . (8:1-22).

Even though the flood destroys all of mankind and
all of the animals on the earth, God allows Noah and
his family to be spared in order to begin again. Clearly
there is a moral purpose to the flood. Noah is the excep-

tion to the destruction. Even Peter argues that Noah and his family were spared due to the righteous character of the great patriarch: "For if God . . . did not spare the ancient world, but preserved Noah, a preacher of righteousness, with seven others, when He brought a flood upon the world of the ungodly" (2 Peter 2:5). If Noah is spared because of his right relationship with God, it is evident that all of those who were destroyed did not have a right relationship with God.

Noah and his family build an altar to the Lord, which pleases God: ". . . and the Lord said to Himself, 'I will never again curse the ground on account of man, . . . and I will never again destroy every living thing, as I have done' " (8:21).

> And God blessed Noah and his sons and said to them, "Be fruitful and multiply, and fill the earth. . . . Only you shall not eat flesh with its life, that is, its blood. . . . Now behold, I Myself do establish My covenant with you, and with your descendants after you; . . . I set My bow in the cloud, . . ." (9:1-17).

God reaffirms man's dominion over the earth. He allows man to eat meat but not blood. God prohibits the taking of a man's life because every man has the honor of being made in God's image. God's covenant is an everlasting promise that He will never again destroy the earth by water. The rainbow serves as His constant symbol of His faithfulness to His covenant with man. As in the beginning, it is God who initiates a relationship with mankind. Due to God's grace and faithfulness this new relationship has possibilities through the covenant that God ordained.

> Now the sons of Noah who came out of the ark were Shem and Ham and Japheth; . . . So all the days of Noah were nine hundred and fifty years, and he died (9:18-29).

These verses seem to answer the question, Why is it that nations are unequal to one another? Why are the

Canaanites so disliked by the Jews? The answer of this text is that Noah was lying in his tent, and Ham came in and saw his father's nakedness. He told his two brothers, who walked in the tent backwards and covered Noah. When Noah woke up, he blessed his two sons who had covered him and cursed the descendants of Ham who were the Canaanites. The instance of Noah's drunkenness serves as the story to explain certain later relationships between the Jews and other nations.

> Now these are the records of the generations of Shem, Ham, and Japheth, . . . These are the families of the sons of Noah, according to their genealogies, by their nations; and out of these the nations were separated on the earth after the flood (10:1-32).

This section of Scripture constitutes a marvelous historic document. It shows the relationship of the Jews to the various nations of the earth. It mentions cities, some of which have been excavated and some which have not. For instance, scholars do not know the identity of Resen (v. 12). This section also sets the stage for explaining how a common language must have existed so that men would later be able to build the Tower of Babel. Finally, this table of nations begins to focus on the Semites which is the family of origin for Nahor, Terah, and Abram. This sets the stage for understanding the beginning of Jewish history with the life of Abram. Rather than being a dry and uninteresting section of Scripture, this text turns out to be one of the most fascinating documents in Genesis.

CONCLUSION

The flood is one of those historic moments which defies description and understanding. It was such a colossal event that there is no way to completely understand all of its ramifications. It is important to understand that the Lord Jesus Christ Himself uses the flood and the moral lifestyle which it destroyed to warn us regarding our current relationship with God. Notice the Lord's words in Luke 17:26, 27: "And just as it happened in the days of Noah, so it shall be also in the days of the Son of Man: they were eating, they were drinking, they were marrying, they were being given in marriage, until the day that Noah entered the ark, and the flood came and destroyed them all." The force of Jesus' warning to the wicked concerns the coming doom of the final days of Judgment. There is a certain ultimate finality about the argument of Christ and the flood that He uses as His illustrations. In short, the flood is one of those very special moments in God's dealings with man which causes us to think soberly about our relationship with Him. In the flood there were swirling waters of death signifying God's justice, but there were also a raven and a dove symbolizing God's grace.

QUESTIONS

1. Describe a world without God.

2. How has God's creation missed the mark before the flood?

3. What is the point of the flood?

4. How does God demonstrate His love in the flood?

5. What does the flood signify about man's special relationship with God?

Abram's Call: A Man in Motion

It is known as "Type A Personality." Modern psychology describes such a person as always on the move, assertive, stress-oriented, aggressive, and highly active. The phrase describes lots of modern-day people whose lives are spent in the "rat race" of daily living. Stress-induced diseases often come to "Type A" individuals. Such personality traits can be found in both sexes, all races, and belonging to all ethnic groups.

"Always being on the move" is an accurate way to describe the life of Abram, a great Old Testament patriarch, whom we meet in Genesis 12. Abram is always going somewhere.

> By faith Abraham, when he was called, obeyed by going out to a place which he was to receive for an inheritance; and he went out, not knowing where he was going. By faith he lived as an alien in the land of promise, as in a foreign land, dwelling in tents with Isaac and Jacob, fellow heirs of the same promise; for he was looking for the city which has foundations, whose architect and builder is God (Hebrews 11:10).

No wonder Dan Ivans includes Abraham in his book. Ivans describes Abraham:

More than a mere traveler, a transient who rest-
lessly wandered from one oasis to the next. He was
a man with a vision, who worshiped a God who
said, "Go," and "He went," and continued to
"Journey on." Abraham experienced a call from
God and responded to it by faith, which lead to his
struggle with transition.[1]

ABRAHAM, THE FRIEND OF GOD

With the person of Abraham we enter the epic of
the Hebrew people. His family in Mesopotamia is
Aramean. He migrated in nomadic fashion from
Northwest Mesopotamia to the land of Canaan,
where he had contacts with Shechem, the only city
in that part of Central Palestine at that time.[2]

Origins are critical. The TV show entitled "Roots"
caused a great response because it touched the quest in
every person to track his or her identity. Being told that
one's origin is slime and one's destiny is annihilation
causes modern man to have no sense of meaning or
direction. So the Bible is clear in giving us the "Roots"
of Abram. His father is Terah who leaves Ur of the
Chaldeans to go to Canaan. ". . . they went as far as
Haran, and settled there" (11:31).

Now the Lord said to Abram, "Go forth from
your country, and from your relatives and from
your father's house, to the land which I will show
you" (12:1).

Abram's entire life is one of being in motion. His faith
in God is more like a ship at full mast than a rock buried
in a cliff. Abram is an excellent example of Paul Tour-
nier's metaphor of the trapeze—the feeling of suspension in mid-air in between letting go of one bar and
reaching for the next one. Abram experiences this

---

[1]Dan Ivans, *God's People in Transition* (Nashville: Broadman
Press, 1981), 30.

[2]Cyrus Gordon, *The Ancient Near East* (New York: W. W. Norton & Co., 1965), 117.

moment of mid-air suspension when a person must wait for God to act next.

> "And I will make you a great nation, and I will bless you, and make your name great; and so you shall be a blessing; and I will bless those who bless you, and the one who curses you I will curse, and in you all the families of the earth shall be blessed" (12:2, 3).

I am so fortunate to have the notes that my own father wrote on this passage while he fought tuberculosis (1954-55) in the Middle Tennessee Tuberculosis Hospital. As my dad struggled with his faith, he writes of Abram who struggled with his own faith. Dad points out, "The call of Abram was manifestly Divine. The patriarch did not by study and meditation discover the duty which he afterward obeyed. The idea did not arise in his own mind, but was suggested to him from a source purely Divine. Saint Stephen says that 'the God of glory appeared unto our father Abraham.'

"Abram's call could not have been an illusion, for to obey it he gave up all that was dear and precious to him in the world. He gave up country, home, friends, and entered upon an untried path, committing himself to unknown chances. Furthermore, the course of conduct he followed could not be of human suggestion. Abram was not driven from his country by adverse circumstances or attracted by the promise of plenty elsewhere. Natural causes cannot account for so sudden and marked change.

"Abram's call demanded great sacrifices. With no human prospect of compensation, he had to sever the ties of country. It is natural for a man to love his native land, the scenes of his earliest years and first impressions. His country becomes hallowed over the years by tender associations. Abram also had to sever the ties of kindred. Natural relationships form a strong bond of unity and awaken a peculiar love. A man must have a stronger affection for his own flesh and blood than the

rest of the human race. He clings with a fond attach-
ment to those who were the guardians of early life. He
also had to sever the ties of home. This is more narrow
than kindred and signifies all the dear and precious
things that form our domestic circle or lie nearest our
hearts. A man has an instinctive belief in a home, a
sacred spot where he can find rest and comfort and be
secure from invasion."

> So Abram went forth as the Lord had spoken to
> him; and Lot went with him. Now Abram was
> seventy-five years old when he departed from
> Haran (12:4).

My dad observes that this is a great example of faith.
"God's promise was made in general terms and the
good things to come, as far as Abram was personally
concerned, placed at an inaccessible distance. Faith is
required to brave the terrors of the unknown. Abraham
went forth upon his untried journey without any clear
idea as to where he was going or what might await him
along the course. The unknown is ever the terrible and
we can only pursue it with confidence or hope when
supported by the power of faith. Consider Abram's
faith. He places his trust in God. Abraham did not
know where he was going, but like Paul, he knew
'whom he had believed.' Religion does not require us to
exercise a blind faith. Often, reason will be present
enough to give us some understanding. But we have to
venture something and that something is trust in God."
    The faith of Abram necessitates the risk of adven-
ture. If faith does not include adventure, it is not faith
at all. If faith can see each step of the path, it is sight,
not faith. Like Abram, it is often necessary for us to step
out, trusting only God, not really knowing what lies
ahead. No wonder Abram has come to symbolize great
faith. Whenever you and I come to a crossroad, Abram
is already standing there giving us his life example of
faith and trust in God.

> And the Lord appeared to Abram and said, "To
> your descendants I will give this land." So he built
> an altar there to the Lord who had appeared to him
> (12:7).

The call of Abram is accompanied by a great promise. My dad writes that "God does not explain all of the
reasons for His dealings to believers. He does not show
them every step of the way in which they shall be led,
yet He gives them sufficient encouragement by the
promise of future good."

Notice that God does not promise the land to Abram
himself but to his "offspring." Land represents a place,
a sacred trust, an opportunity. But Abram will never
know such a place because he will always be on the
move. Uncertainty and lack of place characterize
Abram's life. Even though God's promise to Abram
was never completed in his lifetime, Abram did not
abandon his trust in God's promise. His response to
God's promise and his entering into an eternal covenant with God leads him to worship. His "altar there to
the Lord" is a token of the agreement with God and his
adoration of God. The very closeness of Abram to God
and God to Abram is necessary if we are to understand
Genesis. In modern times, if a man claims to have
talked with God, he would probably be committed to a
mental hospital. From the biblical viewpoint, it is not
so strange for God to appear to men such as Abram.
The result is covenant and worship.

ABRAM'S BLIND SPOT (12:10-20)

> Now there was a famine in the land; so Abram
> went down to Egypt to sojourn there, for the fam-
> ine was severe in the land (12:10).

This verse introduces into the call of Abram the story
of Abram's humanity. Sometimes people think that
God does not work in a life that commits sin or that God
cannot be present in an immoral life. But these ideas

fall apart when one reads the next several verses describing Abram's life. "Famine" is the way to describe the barren, dry, fruitless experience of Abram in Egypt.

> . . . "See now, I know that you are a beautiful woman; . . . Please say that you are my sister so that it may go well with me because of you, and that I may live on account of you" (12:11, 13).

Abram waivers between certainty and uncertainty, faith and doubt, security and insecurity. Abram must have frequently asked himself, "How can I be sure that God will take care of me? How can I know? Is not the king of Egypt more powerful than God Himself? Suppose God forgets to provide care and concern for me while I am in Egypt. What will happen to me then?" Do these questions sound familiar? They are filled with doubt, confusion, worry, and anxiety. Whenever we face the unknown, the untried, and the uncertain, it is easy to rush down to Egypt and to rely upon ourselves rather than upon God. Abram is not perfect. More than once he struggles with doubt, fear, and uncertainty. So a great biblical truth surfaces: God never gives up on Abram, though Abram is a sinner. The New Testament is filled with examples, like Peter and Paul, of those who struggle with their faith and their doubts, but God never gave up on them. What a great Father and what great love He has for us!

> And it came about when Abram came into Egypt, the Egyptians saw that the woman was very beautiful. . . . and the woman was taken into Pharaoh's house. Therefore he treated Abram well for her sake; . . . (12:14-16).

Abram stops trusting God, panics during the famine, gets quickly down to Egypt where food abounds, and momentarily loses his faith. In an effort to make a good impression upon the Egyptians, Abram is willing to sacrifice Sarai to the Egyptians. In fact, he reasons that by allowing Pharaoh to take her, Pharaoh will treat him with great favor. His reasoning is correct and Pharaoh gives great gifts to Abram.

> But the Lord struck Pharaoh and his house with great plagues because of Sarai, Abrams' wife. . . . "Why did you not tell me that she was your wife?" (12:17, 18).

In an effort to carry out His will, the Lord brings horrible diseases on Pharaoh's household. How Pharaoh figures out that the diseases are the result of having Sarai in his harem, the text does not make clear. But the text clearly shows that Pharaoh possesses either great self-interest or a high moral code because he challenges Abram with the questions, "What have you done to me?" and, "Why didn't you tell me she was your wife?" Numerous ancient societies made adultery an illegal act and one capable of severe punishment. In short, Pharaoh returns Sarai to Abram after having rebuked the great man of faith for his deception.

> And Pharaoh commanded his men concerning him; and they escorted him away, with his wife and all that belonged to him (12:20).

Genuine faith is fought out in the lands of Egypt under severe test and trial. Faith is not a set of neat answers to difficult questions, but it is urging us to go forward with God into an unknown future. As God works through Pharaoh, He protects the lives of Abram and Sarai for whom He has great plans and great hopes.

CRUCIAL LESSONS

The call of Abram suggests some powerful eternal truths which cannot be overlooked and which have to surface from this section of Genesis.

First, the call of Abram reveals the grace of God. Abram did not choose God, but God chose Abram. There is nothing in Abram to recommend him to God.

The basis of God's choice lies in God's everlasting mercy and grace. That same grace allows us the opportunity to be the children of Abram.

Second, the call of Abram is authoritative. The authority cannot be questioned. There is a clear revelation from God Himself. There is no room for debate though there is room for disobedience. While the city-states of the surrounding cultures sink into idolatry, Abram hears the clear clarion call of the eternal God.

Third, obedience is painful. The response of Abram to the call of God is not easy. It takes Abram away from everything that he has known and begins a journey through untried experiences. There is no way for Abram to know the turns in the road or the destination of his journey. At best, he must exercise daily faith in following this God who has called him.

My dad wrote from his hospital bed many years ago this conclusion: "A similar command is virtually given to us. We are not called to leave our country and connections but to withdraw our affections from earthly things and fix them upon things above. The world around us lies in wickedness; we are not to love it or things that are in it; we are rather to come out from it and to be crucified to it. We are to fulfill our pilgrimage to heaven in the same spirit as did Abram."

QUESTIONS

1. In what sense is Abram "always on the move"?

2. How does the fate of Abram necessitate adventure and risk?

3. Is it possible for a person to be faithful and uncertain?

4. What is Abram's blind spot?

5. What eternal truths does "the call of Abram" suggest?

6   Genesis 13—15

Abram's Righteousness

The desert at night can be awesome. As the sun sinks in the west, the pastels begin to turn into greys. The greys turn into the dark; it becomes a time of stillness and a time of quiet. The night in the desert is usually silent. An occasional wind bursts the silence. The stars are countless in a clear sky. Most of the animals sleep. All is quiet.

I suppose that it was on just such an evening that Abram stood by his tent flap and wondered what in the world he had come to know? Who is leading him? After all, in a culture that worshiped fire, air, water, the soil, and the sun, Abram uniquely got hold of the notion of God. Adam Clarke believes that the citizens of Ur worshiped fire "and in that place this sort of worship probably originated."[1] Why he, like many other chieftains of his world, did not worship the elements of the earth, we will never quite know. But in this world of polytheism, in this world in which men are groping to worship something bigger than themselves to get an understanding of themselves, a man by the name of Abram

---

[1] Adam Clarke, *The Holy Bible With a Commentary and Critical Notes*, vol. 1, *Genesis to Deuteronomy* (New York: Abingdon Press, n.d.), 92.

gets hold of the notion of the *one* God. He has no Bible. He has never heard of Jesus. He cannot go back inside his tent and begin to read from the books of the Old or New Testament. He cannot sit down and begin to work through the Ten Commandments. It is four hundred years before those Commandments are even given. Uniquely and surprisingly Abram gets hold of the notion of the living, merciful God.

In 14:13, he is called "Abram the Hebrew," a term which Cyrus Gordon interprets as "marking a clean break with his Aramean past."[2] Clearly, Abram's family roots in Mesopotamia are Aramean. They speak Aramaic (31:47), and they are known as Arameans (25:20; 28:5; 31:20). By 14:19, Melchizedek blesses Abram as a follower of God Most High. Abram and his family worship God.

GENESIS 15

On this particular night as God is working with Abram, He calls Abram outside his tent. God tells Abram that Eliezer will not be his heir. God promises a son. Even though Sarai is barren and cannot have children and though Abram's body "is as good as dead," God promises a son. He leads Abram outside his tent and tells him that his descendants will be as many as the stars in the desert sky.

> Then he believed in the Lord; and He reckoned it to
> him as righteousness (15:6).

Abram has not even held the notion of God very long. Now the textbook raises the question, "How will Abram be right with this God?" There is one thing you can say about the Bible, it does not waste any time getting to the paramount issues. Why, he has not any more than

---

[2]Cyrus Gordon, *The Ancient Near East* (New York: W. W. Norton & Co., 1965), 117.

come to the notion that there is a God, until the question is raised, "How will he be right with this God? How is one saved with this God? How does one come into a condition of acceptance with this God? How does one come in right relationship with this God?"

BASIS OF SALVATION: MERIT?

The text explores that maybe, just possibly, it is by Abram's and Sarai's own effort. Maybe the way in which you are right with God, the way in which you become saved with this God, maybe the way in which you have a correct relationship with this one God is that you do it yourself. Perhaps, one can do it on the basis of his own human effort. Now, that is a possibility. And it is a possibility always when one is beginning to raise the question, "How do I become right with this one God?" That is not only a possibility with some; it has become, in fact, their own theory of salvation. Religion is always open to human pride. In the New Testament, the Pharisee takes his fist, beats his breast, looks over at the sinner, and thanks God he is not like the sinner. He claims his good works of fasting, praying, and keeping the law. He tries to save himself by his own merit. I am coming into a right relationship with this one God, based upon what I do. Not only is this a possibility, this is something that many religious people have tried.

But there is a real problem here: Abram and Sarai cannot produce a son on their own. Abram is ninety-nine years old. The text describes his body as "good as dead." He sexually cannot impart his seed to Sarai, and if he did at the age of ninety-nine, the text says she is "barren." She cannot conceive. If you are asking, "How do you get right with this God, and how do you please this God?" and your answer is "By my own effort," the problem with that is not a theoretical one but a practical one. Abram and Sarai just cannot do it on their own.

He is too old and she is barren.

BASIS OF SALVATION: FAITH

The text begins to move to another possibility of being right with this God. The Word of God says, "Do you want to know the principle upon which this man becomes right with this God? Do you want to know the basis on which he becomes acceptable to God? Do you want to know how he is saved?" "Then he believed in the Lord; and He reckoned it to him as righteousness" (15:6).

Thank the Lord for the other way! Praise the Lord that salvation does not depend on our own human effort, on the basis of our own work, ingenuity, education, or religious deeds. The way is on the basis of trust. Abram will have children. Can he count the stars? That is how many descendants he will have. It will not come through Eliezer. It will not come through a manservant. It will not come through a maidservant. It will come from his own flesh. It will come from Sarai. There is God's promise to Abram. And, Abram trusts God to do what nature cannot. He places his faith in God. Faith responds to grace. "And He reckoned it to him as righteousness."

Notice the companion passage in the New Testament: "What then shall we say that Abraham, our forefather according to the flesh, has found?" (Romans 4:1). There is the question again. Not only did Abraham get hold of God, but of a loving God. How does one please God? "For if Abraham was justified by works, he has something to boast about; but not before God" (Romans 4:2). If he and Sarai could have had their children by themselves, they would not need God. "For what does the Scripture say? 'And Abraham believed God, and it was reckoned to him as righteousness' " (Romans 4:3). Verses 13 through 16a continue quoting from Genesis 15:

For the promise to Abraham or to his descendants
that he would be heir of the world was not through
the Law, but through the righteousness of faith.
For if those who are of the Law are heirs, faith is
made void and the promise is nullified; for the Law
brings about wrath, but where there is no law,
neither is there violation. For this reason it is by
faith. . . .

Do you hear that God tells Abraham that He will send
children? They will be as numberless as the stars.
Father Abraham believes God can do it. Faith responds
to grace. Continuing in Romans 4:16: ". . . that it might
be in accordance with grace, in order that the promise
may be certain to all the descendants, not only to those
who are of the Law, but also to those who are of the
faith of Abraham. . . ." We need to continue to thank
God that we can be the children of Abraham. Are we
Jews? Of course not. We are not children of Abraham
through the law; we are children of Abraham through
faith. God says to us that He will forgive us our sins if
we accept the blood of Jesus. He will take us home to
live with Him if we will be faithful unto death. He will
answer our prayers if we will but seek, ask, and knock.
He makes the promise. Response to the God of promises
is the response of trust. It is the response of faith.

Abram becomes, in principle, the great example of
what you and I are doing today. The way in which we
become right with God is not by our own human effort
but by our daily trust in the grace of God. Abram is
right with God. When did this happen? When was it
that God said, "Abram, I have saved you. You are right
with Me. I accept you"? That is a difficult question.
Here is the issue. Was it done after he was circumcised
or before he was circumcised? The answer has severe
implications. If Abraham was saved after his circumcision, only Jews are saved. Now all can get in on
salvation. All the Gentiles have a chance at salvation if
he was right with his God before he was circumcised. It

is a critical question and one that the Word of God not only raises in the Old Testament, but also in the New.

The man Abraham is accounted as right with his God two chapters before he is circumcised. It is not a matter of being circumcised that saves. Circumcision cannot become a merit on which to rest salvation.

Any obedience does not provide the ground for salvation. though obedience always takes place in a person's life when he is right with God.

In Romans 4:9-12, Paul teaches regarding the circumcision of Abraham.

> Is this blessing then upon the circumcised, or upon the uncircumcised also? [Is this being right with God, is this wonderful state of being accepted by God only for the circumcised?] For we say, "Faith was reckoned to Abraham as righteousness." How then was it reckoned? While he was circumcised, or uncircumcised? [Was it after he was circumcised or before?] Not while circumcised, but while uncircumcised; and he received the sign of circumcision, a seal of the righteousness of the faith which he had while uncircumcised, that he might be the father of all who believe without being circumcised, that righteousness might be reckoned to them, and the father of circumcision to those who not only are of the circumcision, but who also follow in the steps of the faith of our father Abraham which he had while uncircumcised.

So the question of when he becomes right with God becomes a critical question in the Word both in the Old and New Testaments. The Word makes clear that God accepted Abraham before his circumcision so that it could always be understood that the principle of being right with God is a personal trust in this great God.

CONCLUSION

I just received a copy of an old letter written almost fifty years ago by my great-grandmother. In her old age, she read the Bible on a daily basis just as she had done earlier in her life. "I have read six chapters in 1 Samuel. Have read Genesis, Exodus, Leviticus, Numbers, Deuteronomy, Joshua, Judges, Ruth and my lesson tomorrow is chapter 7 of 1 Samuel. I am glad I like to read the Old as well as the New." For centuries, people have been attracted to the Old and New Testaments because they tell the same story. It is the story of man's salvation. Man's faith responds to God's grace.

QUESTIONS

1. Where does Abram get his notion about God (especially in view of his culture)?

2. Explain the difference between merit and fate as a basis of salvation.

3. In what sense are *we* not children of Abraham, and in what sense are *we* children of Abram?

4. At what point is Abram right with God?

5. How does Paul interpret Abram's righteousness with God?

A New Name: Abram to Abraham

THE HUMAN NEED

Everyone who knew Abram and Sarai had expected them to have children, but they did not expect that anymore. Other men and women of a similar kind of occupation and status were having children, but no longer did people expect it to be natural. Everyone used to say it would happen, but no one said it would happen anymore. It was now a subject of great embarrassment.

A Sense of Failure

Sarai must have looked down and felt like the dirt that she saw underneath her sandals as she walked across the desert. Whenever she opened her tent flap and saw the dust bounce into the air, she must have felt of no more value than the dust. She must have felt a deep sense of pain and failure. In antiquity, for a man to not be able to have children was considered a curse. Ancients thought of children as gifts of the gods. So Aristotle defines "happiness" as including "plenty of children."[1] For a woman to be barren made her of no

---

[1] Aristotle, *Rhetoric*, trans. W. Rhys Roberts (New York: Modern Library, 1954), 38.

real importance, and she felt that lack of value as well as low self-esteem.

I suppose that is just the way Abram and Sarai felt after trying to have children for many, many years and never having any. Sarai was barren, disgraced, shunned, and felt terrible low self-esteem. Abram's body was, as the Scripture says, "good as dead." It was not that they had not tried; they had tried many times. Romance had been there. I am sure they had tried to make themselves appealing to one another many, many times, physically and sexually, but it had paid no dividends for them. They had tried valiantly and failed. They did not have the ability to produce children. If children were born to them, it would come from another source. They had failed.

God Promises

At this very moment God comes to Abram and makes him the most unbelievable promise you could ever imagine! He promises him the great land—the land of Canaan—but that is not the promise that the Scripture discusses in detail. He promises Abram a son, and He says this son will come from Abram and Sarai. From that son would be an enormous number of descendants—a huge number of people. God refers Abram to the sky and challenges him to count the stars. That is how many will be in his great ancestry. Numberless people in the ancestry of Abraham and Sarah and both are failures at producing children!

Both of them are barren, impotent, and physically unable by their own performance to bring about a son; so God promises Abram and Sarai a son. This raises important questions. What is it God is seeking from Abram under these peculiar conditions? Is God looking for performance? Or something else? Is He looking for perfection? Surely He is not. Abraham, we will shortly see, is a liar on some occasions—when his own self-interest is at stake. God certainly is not looking for holiness and perfection on the part of two human beings. What is God looking for? What is God always looking for when He makes a promise? When God makes you and me a promise, what is it He is looking for in us? It is the same thing He is looking for in Abram and Sarai. He is looking for great, great faith on the part of Abram and Sarai. He is looking for trust in God. He is looking for reliance now upon Himself. There can be no more reliance on each of them since they cannot do it, but great trust, reliance, and faith in the God who makes the promise. God is seeking exactly what Abram gives—faith, trust, and reliance.

A VITAL PRINCIPLE

Here is the great biblical truth: *Promises require faith.* The promises of God require the faith of Abram and Sarai. Abram's faith is clearly being built on two factors: (1) the importance of Sarai and himself to have any children, their deep awareness of their own dead bodies, and their own inability to do what God wants them to do; and (2) the power of God to fulfill the promise He makes. So here is the remarkable faith of Abram.

In 15:6, when Abram believes the Lord, when this promise is given by God to Abram and Abram believes it . . . at that moment Abram enters into a right relationship with God.

> Then he believed in the Lord; and He reckoned it to
> him as righteousness.

Clearly, this is before the circumcision of Abram which is in Genesis 17. Certainly, it is before the law of Moses—it is 430 years before the law is given. On what principle does Abram come into right relationship with God? It cannot be on his own performance because he is physically unable to have children, as is Sarai. It cannot be on virtue. It cannot be on perfection. It cannot be on works. It cannot be on law. It can only be on one principle. God accepts Abram into a right relationship with Him based on Abram's faith.

GOD PROMISES AND MAN BELIEVES (17)

> Now when Abram was ninety-nine years old, the Lord appeared to Abram and said to him, "I am God Almighty; walk before Me, and be blameless. And I will establish My covenant between Me and you, and I will multiply you exceedingly." And Abram fell on his face, and God talked with him, saying, "As for Me, behold, My covenant is with you, and you shall be the father of a multitude of nations. No longer shall your name be called Abram, but your name shall be Abraham; for I will make you the father of a multitude of nations" (17:1-5).

Why does God change their names? It seems like such a small thing. But you will remember many instances in which the name of a person in the Word of God is very important. Sometimes the name of a person gives a physical description of the person. The name Esau means "hairy." The name that he was given depicts his physical appearance. Sometimes the name refers to a person's personality. Do you remember the name "Jacob"? It means "deceiver" or "cheater." Then his name is later changed to "Israel," meaning "chosen" or "beloved" of God. After he had finally faced the fact that he could no longer get his way in this world by cheating and deceiving, he realized that the only dependable one is God. Sometimes a name depicts an event. The name Moses means "drawn out of the water." Moses was drawn out in the basket of bullrushes as a little baby. It was an event. But God changes Abram's and Sarai's names for a different reason. It has nothing to do with their appearance or personality. What is God doing here when He changes their names? At least five things are going on in this name change that are crucial. They are found in Genesis 17.

First, Abraham and Sarah now have a new relationship with God (see 15:6). Abraham has a new relationship with God, and this new name helps depict that new relationship. He needs a new name to adequately describe the destiny that God has for him. God says, in effect, "Abraham, I have great hopes for you. I have great dreams for you. You will be the father of many nations. In order to depict that destiny for you, I'm giving you a new name. You will no longer be Abram, the exalted father; you will be Abraham, the father of many nations." Is that not also true for you? God has a great destiny for you. God has a great relationship that you are in. If you have been baptized into Jesus Christ, you are in that right relationship with Him. You came into that relationship on the basis of your faith in His promise. You believe that promise just as Abram did, and God gave you a new name—Christian. You have a new name because you have a new destiny, and God has great plans for you.

Second, Abraham and Sarah have a new covenant with God. God loves covenants, does He not? God is always making covenants with people. He made a covenant with Noah; He told Noah He would give him a sign. God says, "I will change your name. I will make you fruitful. I will establish My covenant which will be everlasting. The whole land of Canaan will be yours as an eternal or everlasting possession." Then He gives him a sign of the covenant, and that sign (17:9) is the sign of circumcision.

> "And you shall be circumcised in the flesh of your foreskin; and it shall be the sign of the covenant between Me and you. And every male among you who is eight days old shall be circumcised throughout your generations, . . ." (17:11, 12).

Third, Abraham has this new sign of a relationship which is circumcision (17:9-14). Circumcision, Paul argues in Romans 4, is not a condition of the justification of Abraham. He does not become circumcised to please God and to be right with God. He is already right with God. Circumcision is a sign of the covenant that he now has with God. It is a sign of his justification.

Fourth, Abraham has a new mission now in life. He is no longer just a nomad. He is a patriarch of many, many nations. Romans 4:11, 12 says, "And he [speaking of Abraham] received the sign of circumcision, a seal of the righteousness of the faith which he had while uncircumcised,..." He gets right with God on the basis of his faith. Then he is circumcised as a sign of the new relationship with Him. God gives him a new mission. It continues: "... that he might be the father of all who believe without being circumcised, that righteousness might be reckoned to them." So here is this marvelous name that is given to Abraham signifying his new mission. He is no longer going to be the father of a boy. He is going to be the father of a nation of people who come to God on the principle of faith.

Fifth, Abraham now gives all the glory to God. He has a new name. Why does he have a new name? He has a new name so he can give all the glory to God. "Abram" means "exalted father, patriarch, upstanding, fine man." But Abraham has new meaning and purpose. God has to go to work now to produce many, many descendants. Abraham gives the glory to God. Paul continues his thought in Romans 4:16, 17 by saying that,

> ... Abraham, who is the father of us all, (as it is written, "A father of many nations have I made you") in the sight of Him whom he believed, even God, who gives life to the dead and calls into being that which does not exist.

CONCLUSION

Look at your own life. Do you remember when you were dead? Do you remember when you were impotent?

Do you remember when you were like Sarai, like Abram? Do you remember what guilt did to you? Do you remember that you just could not do enough, and the more you tried, the more you failed? You were dead in your sins. But Christ came and gave His blood for you, and you believed in Him. You accepted Him. Your faith produced obedience. You came to Him and on the same basis of a trusting, acting faith, God credited it to you as righteousness and gave you a new name, and that new name signifies all to you that it did to Abraham. Wear that name of Christ with both humility and pride. You belong to Him.

QUESTIONS

1. What condition caused Sarai to feel a deep sense of inadequacy and failure?

2. How does God take this moment and turn it into a moment for spiritual growth?

3. What is the great biblical truth regarding promises?

4. What is the significance of the new name as given by God?

5. How does Abraham's life typify your own life?

Laughter, Intercession, And Deliverance

The Danish theologian, Soren Kierkegaard, tells an interesting story about a man who escapes from an insane asylum and faces the very real prospect that he will be recognized as insane and returned to the hospital. He decides to disguise his insanity by uttering some generally accepted truth that would prove that he was sane. He found a rubber ball and began to bounce the ball on the street; and as he met any particular person who would come toward him, he would begin to say, "The earth is round. The earth is round. The earth is round." Needless to say he was immediately recognized as insane and returned to the asylum. Why is that true? Why was he immediately recognized as insane? He was stating something that was obviously true. The earth is round. You, of course, know the answer to the question. There is something very nonsensical about a person who utters a truth but the participation in that truth has no effect whatsoever on his life. The point that Kierkegaard made is certainly a point that is made in Genesis.

The story of Abraham is a crucial story because of the very point made by Kierkegaard. Here is a man whose life is affected by the truth that he is speaking. He is very affected by this God he has discovered and in whom he has great, great faith.

THE LAUGHTER (18:1-15)

The Lord appeared to Abraham near the great oak trees of Mamre while he was sitting at the entrance to his tent in the heat of the day. Those great oak trees of Mamre are still living today. Imagine Abraham sitting under those great trees, perhaps dozing in the heat of the day.

> And when he lifted up his eyes and looked, behold, three men were standing opposite him; . . . (18:2).

There is no indication that Abraham thinks they are heavenly visitors. They are, but Abraham does not consider it strange that three men suddenly appear coming toward him.

> . . . and when he saw them, he ran from the tent door to meet them, and bowed himself to the earth.

"Bowed" is not a term of worship. This is simply an ancient act of courtesy. Abraham then says,

> My lord, if now I have found favor in your sight, please do not pass your servant by (18:3).

Abraham does not want to pass by the opportunity of sharing a blessing. He says,

> Please let a little water be brought and wash your feet, and rest yourselves under the tree; and I will bring a piece of bread, that you may refresh your-selves; after that you may go on, since you have visited your servant. . . . (18:4, 5).

Abraham wants to share some of his water and food. It will not deprive him of his necessities. This is genuine hospitality on the part of Abraham. It is mentioned in 19:2; 24:32; and 43:24. Hospitality is one of the great attributes of the people of God. Abraham's hospitality is especially an example to modern-day followers of Christ.

> So Abraham hurried into the tent to Sarah, and said, "Quickly, prepare three measures of fine flour, knead it, and make bread cakes." Abraham also ran to the herd, and took a tender and choice calf, and gave it to the servant; and he hurried to prepare it (18:6, 7).

Notice he is an old man, but he runs out to the herd. Abraham is always running. He does not want his guests to have to wait. He wants the finest meat prepared for his guests.

> And he took curds and milk and the calf which he had prepared, and placed it before them; . . . (18:8).

He has prepared a real feast. He has genuinely opened up his tents to these visitors.

> . . . and he was standing by them under the tree as they ate.

Here is a gesture of the highest courtesy that he could pay to his guests. He does not sit down to eat with them. He stands under a tree. A very courteous man, Abraham shows a special awareness of the ancient Middle East courtesies.

> Then they said to him, "Where is Sarah your wife?" . . . (18:9).

This is the first indication we have that these visitors are not human beings. They are asking for Sarah by name, yet her name has not been mentioned in their presence. Abraham said, "Behold, in the tent."

> And he said, "I will surely return to you at this time next year; and behold, Sarah your wife shall have a son" (18:10).

God sometimes appeared in different forms to the ancients (Exodus 3:2, 4; Acts 7:30, 35, 38). God may well be one of the beings that is present with the other two in this conversation.

This is the second time that God directly says Sarah will have a child. God says here that He will come back near the end of her pregnancy when she is due to have that child, and Sarah will have a son.

> ... And Sarah was listening at the tent door, which was behind him. Now Abraham and Sarah were old, advanced in age; Sarah was past childbearing (18:10, 11).

God wants us to understand that the baby is from God, not from Abraham and Sarah. It could not have come from them. Therefore, they can never boast in it, and they will give their praise to God who gave them the son.

> Now Abraham and Sarah were old, advanced in age; Sarah was past childbearing (18:11).

How many times has the text mentioned this?

> And Sarah laughed to herself, saying, "After I have become old, shall I have pleasure, my lord being old also?" (18:12).

Apparently, the Lord had instructed Abraham to tell Sarah about the promise. (See 17:16, 19.) She has been told, but she disbelieves. Therefore, the Lord comes a second time to now assure Abraham and Sarah.

> And the Lord said to Abraham, "Why did Sarah laugh, saying, 'Shall I indeed bear a child, when I am so old?' " (18:13).

Wonder how Sarah's laugh made the Lord feel?

> "Is anything too difficult for the Lord? At the appointed time I will return to you, at this time next year, and Sarah shall have a son" (18:14).

Here she laughs in derision, in disbelief, in cynicism. The Lord exposes Sarah's lack of faith. She tries to avoid it by denying it.

> Sarah denied it however, saying, "I did not laugh";
> ... And he said, "No, but you did laugh" (18:15).

Is it not interesting how we as human beings devise ways to excuse our sins, but He is always ahead of us? We are afraid of being exposed as Sarah was. But the Lord forces her to face her own lack of faith. That is so true for us as human beings; we have such a lack of faith. He causes us to face, responsibly, our lack of faith.

THE INTERCESSION (18:16-33)

The cities of the valley around the southern tip of the Dead Sea were cities like the Garden of Eden. They were lush and beautiful. They had a wide variety of trees. This is the place people wanted to live, and this is the place Lot chose for his family to live because of the water and the lush vegetation. It was all there. But the cities of the valley became so evil that God now decides to destroy them. The destruction begins in the intercession.

> Then the men rose up from there, and looked down toward Sodom; and Abraham was walking with them to send them off (18:16).

Now God and the two angels have a mission. It is to go down into the cities of the valley, Sodom and Gomorrah.

> And the Lord said, "Shall I hide from Abraham what I am about to do" (18:17).

The text no longer is describing what the men and the angels are doing. It is giving us the thought of God: "I love Abraham. Abraham loves Me. I've made a covenant with Abraham. Abraham has had great faith in the promises that I've given him. Shall I now hide from Abraham what I'm about to do to these cities?"

> "Since Abraham will surely become a great and mighty nation, and in him all the nations of the earth will be blessed?" (18:18).

This is the messianic promise.

> "For I have chosen him, in order that he may command his children and his household after him to keep the way of the Lord by doing right-eousness and justice; in order that the Lord may bring upon Abraham what He has spoken about him" (18:19).

Here is a tremendous section for a church, its young people, and parents. God seems to be saying, "I can't keep what I'm about to do from Abraham. I love Abraham. Abraham has loved me and responded in faith. I have to be sure that Abraham understands what I think about evil. I must be sure that Abraham feels the obligation to train his own children to know the way I really think about evil. Now I have to tell him what I will do to evil." This is a tremendous passage that shows us that we as parents are under an obligation to lead our own children to God and to let them know what God thinks of evil in any form. God cannot keep this from Abraham because He wants Abraham to know what He thinks about evil and what is right and just. Surely God's example is a great model for all parents. God's plan for Abraham to guide his own children into His way is a most relevant plan for today's families.

> And the Lord said, "The outcry of Sodom and Gomorrah is indeed great, and their sin is exceed-ingly grave. I will go down now, and see if they have done entirely according to its outcry, which has come to Me; and if not, I will know" (18:20, 21).

The term "outcry" that is used in verse 20 may have one of two meanings. It can mean that the innocent people who have been hurt by the citizens of Sodom and Gomorrah have been hurt for so long that they have cried out to God. Every time a people cry out to God, what does God do? He hears their prayers. God's compassion and grace is touched by the outcry of the hurting. It can also mean that the innocent people in Sodom and Gomorrah are crying out to God. The text is not clear, but there is an outcry coming from people to God about the evil people who live in Sodom and Gomorrah.

> Then the men turned away from there and went toward Sodom, while Abraham was still standing before the Lord (18:22).

Of textual interest here is the phrase "standing before the Lord." It is one of the ancient corrections that the Hebrew scribes made in Genesis. The earlier reading said, "But the Lord stood before Abraham." The Hebrew scribes could not imagine such an event. So they made a correction in the text. Many of the translations will tell us that this is a scribal tradition that has been changed at this point. In any case, God is now willing to listen to Abraham. God is with Abraham, and the other two heavenly beings are going down to Sodom.

> And Abraham came near and said, "Wilt Thou indeed sweep away the righteous with the wicked? Suppose there are fifty righteous within the city; wilt Thou indeed sweep it away and not spare the place for the sake of the fifty righteous who are in it?" . . . So the Lord said, "If I find in Sodom fifty righteous within the city, then I will spare the whole place on their account." . . . "Suppose the fifty righteous are lacking five, wilt Thou destroy the whole city because of five?" . . . (18:23, 24, 26, 28).

Abraham continues to negotiate with the Lord, and then he says finally,

> ". . . suppose ten are found there?" And He said, "I will not destroy it on account of the ten" (18:32).

The chapter ends,

> And as soon as He had finished speaking to Abra-

> ham the Lord departed; and Abraham returned to
> his place (18:33).

Abraham does not see the destruction of the cities. He returns to Mamre. Mamre is south of the Dead Sea. Sodom and Gomorrah are right at the edge and at the end of the southern tip of the Dead Sea. There are beautiful palms, figs, lush gardens, vegetation, animals, and all kinds of people living there. But the crucial thing is what now happens past the intercession.

THE DELIVERANCE (19)

The two angels come to Sodom. Why are they coming? They are looking for ten righteous people. They want to see firsthand if there are ten good people in the city. Here is the expression of God's love. If He can find just ten godly people, He will save the entire valley. But notice that no one even shows them hospitality, which was commonly expected.

> Now the two angels came to Sodom in the eve-
> ning as Lot was sitting in the gate of Sodom. . . .
> (19:1).

In the Old Testament, the gateway of the city served several purposes. For example, in Ruth 4:1 and Amos 5:12, it is at the gate of the city that the ancient judges gave their decisions. The gate of the city is also for legal cases and the handing down of judgments. In Proverbs 31, it is where the elders of the city discussed the activities of the city. So Lot is sitting there; and when he sees them, he gets up and bows down, showing his hospitality. He bows his face to the ground.

> And he said, "Now behold, my lords, please turn
> aside into your servant's house, and spend the
> night, and wash your feet; then you may rise early
> and go on your way." They said however, "No, but
> we shall spend the night in the square." [He does
> not know they are angels.] Yet he urged them
> strongly, so they turned aside to him and entered

his house; and he prepared a feast for them, and baked unleavened bread, and they ate. Before they lay down, the men of the city, the men of Sodom, surrounded the house, both young and old, all the people from every quarter; and they called to Lot and said to him, "Where are the men who came to you tonight? Bring them out to us that we may have relations with them" (19:2-5).

What is occurring here is not some small thing. Moses says every man of the town comes out to see these two visitors. They demand the visitors in order to have sexual relations with them. Homosexuality is condemned throughout all the Old and New Testaments. It is a sin. It can cost a man or woman a soul if the person does not repent of it. It is specifically the practice of homosexuality that is mentioned here in Sodom and Gomorrah that is condemned, and it is condemned everywhere in the Word of God (Leviticus 18:22; 20:13; Romans 1:26, 27; 1 Corinthians 6:9; 1 Timothy 1:10). God's Word condemns gay and homosexual practices. These acts are what brings down any great culture when men and women do not understand the great plan of God in sexuality.

But Lot went out to them at the doorway, and shut the door behind him, and said, "Please, my brothers, do not act wickedly. Now behold, I have two daughters who have not had relations with man; please let me bring them out to you, and do to them whatever you like; only do nothing to these men, inasmuch as they have come under the shelter of my roof." But they said, "Stand aside." Furthermore, they said, "This one came in as an alien [Lot was not born in Sodom so they call him an alien], and already he is acting like a judge; now we will treat you worse than them." So they pressed hard against Lot and came near to break the door. But the men reached out their hands and brought Lot into the house with them, and shut the door. And they struck the men who were at the doorway of the house with blindness, both small and great, so that

> they wearied themselves trying to find the door-
> way (19:6-11).

The language of the text would seem to suggest a blind-
ing flash much like what happened to Saul of Tarsus on
his way to Damascus.

> Then the men said to Lot, "Whom else have you
> here? A son-in-law, and your sons, and your daugh-
> ters, and whomever you have in the city, bring
> them out of the place; for we are about to destroy
> this place, because their outcry has become so
> great before the Lord that the Lord has sent us to
> destroy it." And Lot went out and spoke to his
> sons-in-law, who were to marry his daughters, and
> said, "Up, get out of this place, for the Lord will
> destroy the city." But he appeared to his sons-in-
> law to be jesting (19:12-14).

The time has already been set by God—sunrise. The
two angels are trying to convince Lot to get him and his
family out before sunrise.

> And when morning dawned, the angels urged Lot,
> saying, "Up, take your wife and your two daugh-
> ters, who are here, lest you be swept away in the
> punishment of the city." But he hesitated. So the
> men seized his hand and the hand of his wife and
> the hands of his daughters, for the compassion of
> the Lord was upon him; and they brought him out,
> and put him outside the city (19:15, 16).

This is a story of mercy. The love of God is so great that
He is willing to spare two major cities if He can only
find ten righteous people. In addition, He pleads with
Lot's family so they will not procrastinate their depar-
ture. God sets sunrise as the time He will burn these
cities at the edge of the sea.

> ... "Escape for your life! Do not look behind you,
> and do not stay anywhere in the valley; escape to
> the mountains, lest you be swept away." But Lot
> said to them, "Oh no, my lords! Now behold, your
> servant has found favor in your sight, and you

have magnified your lovingkindness, which you have shown me by saving my life; but I cannot escape to the mountains, lest the disaster overtake me and I die; now behold, this town is near enough to flee to, and it is small. Please, let me escape there (is it not small?) that my life may be saved." And he said to him, "Behold, I grant you this request also, not to overthrow the town of which you have spoken. Hurry, escape there, for I cannot do anything until you arrive there." Therefore the name of the town was called Zoar.

The sun had risen over the earth when Lot came to Zoar. Then the Lord rained on Sodom and Gomorrah brimstone and fire from the Lord out of heaven, and He overthrew those cities, and all the valley, and all the inhabitants of the cities, and what grew on the ground. But his wife, from behind him, looked back; and she became a pillar of salt.

Now Abraham arose early in the morning and went to the place where he had stood before the Lord; and he looked down toward Sodom and Gomorrah, and toward all the land of the valley, and he saw, and behold, the smoke of the land ascended like the smoke of a furnace. Thus it came about, when God destroyed the cities of the valley, that God remembered Abraham, and sent Lot out of the midst of the overthrow, when He overthrew the cities in which Lot lived (19:17-29).

Between verses 17 and 22, God makes five pleas to Lot and his family to leave. Five times he begs them to get out of the city, for dawn is coming. It is the mercy of God. The chapter ends with the incestuous relationship between Lot and his daughters. Apparently, the influence of the culture in which he reared his daughters has overtaken his family in this moment of sin.

CONCLUSION

Sometimes, our culture views the God of the Old Testament as a vicious being who enjoys making His creatures unhappy. But the God of Genesis is full of mercy, love, and grace, and is willing to go to any length to show mankind His true nature. His promises and pleas reveal His genuine nature.

QUESTIONS

1. What caused the laughter?

2. Who interceded and why?

3. Explain the deliverance.

4. What obligation do we as parents have with regard to leading our children?

5. How can God overcome culture?

Isaac at Last

One of the evidences for inspiration of the Scripture is impartiality. When a man writes a book about another man, it is either pro or con. God impartially wrote the book. For example, He tells us not only of the great courage of David, but also of the sins of David.

> The writers of the Bible set forth both the virtues and follies of those of whom they wrote. The lives of both friends and foes were described in a direct, factual manner, rather than in the style found in most literature, where friends are praised and enemies are vilified.[1]

Dr. Baxter cites Abraham in Genesis 20 as an example of God's impartial style in Scripture.

ABRAHAM'S SIN (20)

Genesis 20 is one of the most complicated and complex chapters in the book for a number of reasons. It deals with the sin of one of the greatest men in the Bible. The sin is lying, and the man is Abraham. Second, we are dealing with another culture. We are not

---

[1]Batsell Barrett Baxter, *I Believe Because* . . . (Grand Rapids, Mich.: Baker Book House, 1971), 181.

dealing with Jews and Israelites. We are not dealing with the normal kinds of cultural things that relate to Judaism. We are in another land, another set of mores, another set of cultural norms. Third, it is a very complex chapter because it leaves so many questions open.

Following the destruction of the evil cities, God resumes the story of His promise to Abraham. In effect, God says, "Abraham and Sarah, you will have a son. On what principle and what basis will you have this son? It will not be on the basis of your works or merit." Abraham's body is dead. Sarah is barren. Both are aged, and a son cannot be produced on their own. It would be to their credit. So it will be on a basis other than works. Romans picks up this story and says that it is on the basis of faith and God's promise that a son is going to be born. God will receive the credit. Only God can give them a son. Romans 4:13, 18ff. tells of this incident as Abraham being a great example of faith. We are not dealing with a man who is morally corrupt. We are not dealing with a bad man. We are not dealing with an extremely evil man. Abraham has great faith, but he can also choose to do wrong, and he does.

> Now Abraham journeyed from there toward the land of the Negev, and settled between Kadesh and Shur; . . . (20:1).

We are not sure why Abraham leaves the oaks of Mamre. Perhaps, he is seeking better grazing for the flocks. Or he may be discouraged by the destruction of Sodom, or he may have been threatened by the Canaanite tribes, or he simply may have had the urge to move. Abraham leaves southern Palestine, and he moves almost all the way down to Egypt.

> . . . then he sojourned in Gerar. And Abraham said of Sarah his wife, "She is my sister." So Abimelech king of Gerar sent and took Sarah (20:1, 2).

Here is one of the complicated things about this

chapter. Abimelech, which is a title, is the ruler or king of this small region in the southern Negev. In order to establish a relationship with another person of some wealth and power, it was considered appropriate to marry one of his relatives. The marriage builds an economic and social relationship between the two powers. It is done to establish social, economic, and power relationships. Abimelech thinks that he is marrying the sister of Abraham, because Abraham has said, "This is my sister." That is a half-truth. They are from the same father but not the same mother. What makes it a lie is that it is an intentional effort to deceive. It is not the entire truth. The motive of Abraham is wrong. He is trying to deceive.

> But God came to Abimelech in a dream of the night, and said to him, "Behold, you are a dead man because of the woman whom you have taken, for she is married" (20:3).

Apparently, God gave some kind of disease that prevented the conception of children.

> And Abraham prayed to God; and God healed Abimelech and his wife and his maids, so that they bore children. For the Lord had closed fast all the wombs of the household of Abimelech because of Sarah, Abraham's wife (20:17, 18).

How did God do it? What was the purpose of God's doing it? God frequently opened the wombs and closed the wombs, and He did it out of His own right of sovereignty. Sometimes God prevents evil, and sometimes He promotes good. But we need to remember a tremendous teaching about God that is taking place in this text: It is God's sovereignty, God's power, God's right, and God's decision. How He prevented conception is not clear, but it is clear that He had the right to do it.

> Now Abimelech had not come near her; and he

> said, "Lord, wilt Thou slay a nation, even though
> blameless? Did he not himself say to me, 'She is my
> sister'? And she herself said, 'He is my brother.' In
> the integrity of my heart and the innocence of my
> hands I have done this" (20:4, 5).

Abimelech seems to be saying, "This is our custom,
Lord. We marry a relative in order to have some kind of
social, political, or power relationship. We did not
intend anything else. I did not intend to marry a married woman. It is an innocent nation."

Notice God also talks to people outside His covenant.
He is talking to Abimelech. Abimelech knows who God
is too. Abimelech also knows God, and he fears God. He
fears Him in this instance even more than Abraham.
So many times we get a parochial view that God only
talked to His people in Scripture. But that is wrong.
Abimelech is outside the covenant relationship, but he
is talking to God, and God is talking to him. We will see
that this man fears, worships, and respects God.

Samuel later says God is always looking on the heart.
God is looking on Abimelech's heart, and He is looking
on Abraham's heart. Abimelech's heart is pure. Abraham's heart is not pure. "I have done what I have done
with a clear conscience and with clean hands," claims
Abimelech.

> Then God said to him in the dream, "Yes, I know
> that in the integrity of your heart you have done
> this, and I also kept you from sinning against Me;
> therefore I did not let you touch her" (20:6).

We said that God closed and opened the wombs for
His divine purpose to prevent evil and to promote good.
In effect, God tells Abimelech, "I have kept you from
the temptation of sinning against Me. Because your
heart is right and you did not know that she is a married woman. This is why I did not let you touch her."

> "Now therefore, restore the man's wife, for he is a
> prophet, and he will pray for you, and you will live.

But if you do not restore her, know that you shall surely die, you and all who are yours" (20:7).

He is a prophet in the sense that he has direct access to God. Abimelech can talk to God. God is revealing Himself in a dream to Abimelech at this very moment. So He says to Abimelech, "I want you to know that this man, whose wife you have taken, he is a prophet too. He has direct access to Me as well. He will pray for you, and you will live. Knowing what you now know, Abimelech, it is now your choice. And if you, now knowing that she is a married woman, choose to break the marriage relationship, you and all of yours will die."

> So Abimelech arose early in the morning and called all his servants and told all these things in their hearing; and the men were greatly frightened. Then Abimelech called Abraham and said to him, "What have you done to us? And how have I sinned against you, that you have brought on me and on my kingdom a great sin? You have done to me things that ought not to be done." And Abimelech said to Abraham, "What have you encountered, that you have done this thing?" (20:8-10).

It would appear that there is always a moral understanding that exists between all people. Because we all came from God and there is a moral understanding, a moral code exists. For example, Abimelech seems to be saying, "You are an alien in my country. I let you come into my country. I gave you that kind of privilege and opportunity, and in return you should not have lied to me." (The alien should not lie to the official who has allowed free access to his country.) That is the standard accepted thing. Even today, when aliens come into the United States, we do not appreciate it when they lie to us. It is a commonly accepted moral right.

> And Abraham said, "Because I thought, surely there is no fear of God in this place; and they will kill me because of my wife. Besides, she actually is my sister, the daughter of my father, but not the

daughter of my mother, and she became my wife;
and it came about, when God caused me to wander
from my father's house, that I said to her, 'This is
the kindness which you will show to me: everywhere we go, say of me, "He is my brother." ' "
[God, at this point in history, is allowing marriage
within a family, but that will later be forbidden in
Deuteronomy 27:22.] Abimelech then took sheep
and oxen and male and female servants, and gave
them to Abraham, and restored his wife Sarah to
him. And Abimelech said, "Behold, my land is
before you; settle wherever you please" (20:11-15).

Abimelech can see that this man also fears God, and
he wants to be sure that Abraham knows that he is an
honorable man who also fears and worships God. So,
he brings these gifts. He then brings a gift to Sarah.

And to Sarah he said, "Behold, I have given your
brother a thousand pieces of silver; behold, it is
your vindication before all who are with you, and
before all men you are cleared" (20:16).

Is the sum of "a thousand pieces of silver" the value of
the sheep, cattle, and slaves, or is it an additional
amount? We just know that he is giving gifts to both
Abraham and Sarah, and he is saying to her that she is
completely vindicated.

And Abraham prayed to God; and God healed
Abimelech and his wife and his maids, so that they
bore children. For the Lord had closed fast all the
wombs of the household of Abimelech because of
Sarah, Abraham's wife.

THE BIRTH OF ISAAC (21:1-7)

Then the Lord took note of Sarah as He had said,
and the Lord did for Sarah as He had promised
(21:1).

Here is the story of the birth of Isaac. How Abraham
and Sarah, who are old, trust God! He makes a decision
to bless the nations of the world through Abraham and

Sarah by the birth of Isaac.

> And Sarah said, "God has made laughter for me;
> everyone who hears will laugh with me." And she
> said, "Who would have said to Abraham that
> Sarah would nurse children? Yet I have borne him
> a son in his old age" (21:6, 7).

The word "Isaac" means "he laughed." But who gets
the last laugh? Certainly Abraham laughs. He is full of
joy because Sarah whom he loves so dearly has had a
child. Sarah laughed in derision and unbelief. The
neighbors will laugh when they hear Abraham and
Sarah have had a baby. But what about God? God
probably had the last laugh when He sent Abraham
and Sarah this little boy.

HAGAR AND ISHMAEL SENT AWAY
(21:8-34)

Hagar is the Egyptian handmaiden to Sarah. Abraham and Hagar have a baby by the name of Ishmael.
At the end of the weaning period for Isaac (1 Samuel
indicates three years), Ishmael makes fun of this
moment. Apparently he makes so much fun of it that
the New Testament describes it as no small matter.
"But as at that time he who was born according to the
flesh persecuted him who was born according to the
Spirit, so it is now also" (Galatians 4:29). I do not know
what he did, but whatever he did, it was so terrible that
it made Sarah very upset. She goes to Abraham and
requests that Ishmael and Hagar be sent away. And
Abraham, though he loves Ishmael and Hagar, does
send them away. They go out in the desert toward
Beersheba.

> And the water in the skin was used up, and she left
> the boy under one of the bushes. Then she went
> and sat down opposite him, about a bowshot away,
> for she said, "Do not let me see the boy die." And
> she sat opposite him, and lifted up her voice and

wept (21:15, 16).

God hears the boy crying.

> Then God opened her eyes and she saw a well of
> water; and she went and filled the skin with water,
> and gave the lad a drink (20:19).

**God's will is that He will make a great nation of this
boy.**

> And God was with the lad, and he grew; and he
> lived in the wilderness, and became an archer. And
> he lived in the wilderness of Paran; and his mother
> took a wife for him from the land of Egypt (21:20,
> 21).

Here is God at work. He chooses Isaac over Ishmael.

> But it is not as though the word of God has failed.
> For they are not all Israel who are descended from
> Israel; neither are they all children because they
> are Abraham's descendants, but: "through Isaac
> your descendants will be named" (Romans 9:6, 7).

Who was the natural child of the story in Genesis?
Ishmael. It is not the natural children who are God's
children. It is the children of promise. It is not Ishmael.
It is Isaac. God is in control. God is making the choice.
God writes out the map. If man and woman were doing
it, it would be a natural son done by natural sexual
relationships, and they would get the credit. It is going
to be by the promise of God. Man is going to have to
have faith in God. So Abraham and Sarah do have
faith, and Isaac is given. It will now be through Isaac
that the descendants of the earth will be blessed.

> That is, it is not the children of the flesh who are
> children of God, but the children of the promise are
> regarded as descendants. For this is a word of
> promise: "At this time I will come, and Sarah shall
> have a son" (Romans 9:8, 9).

CONCLUSION

What does this part of "the great story" teach? God is in control of history. God has always been in control. It will ultimately be to the glory of God that history does what it does. In the final analysis, it is God's sovereignty. Whenever we face the sovereignty of God, we have lots of questions. The ultimate answer to every one of them is this: God is working out His will according to His decision. Abraham and Sarah discovered that God can be trusted to do His will. Such trust leads to great joy!

QUESTIONS

1. What was Abraham's sin?

2. How can a man of such great faith choose to do wrong?

3. Tell the story of the birth of Isaac.

4. Why were Hagar and Ishmael sent away?

5. What does this part of "the great story" teach?

A Test, Death, And Joy

"The Lord's lovingkindnesses indeed never cease, for His compassions never fail. They are new every morning; great is Thy faithfulness. 'The Lord is my portion,' says my soul, 'Therefore I have hope in Him' " (Lamentations 3:22-24). There has never been an example of where the faithfulness of God is clearer in the Bible than in Genesis 22, 23, and 24. These three stories demonstrate that God can be trusted. His nature is trustworthy, dependable, and reliable.

THE TEST (22)

I suppose Abraham had not slept any the night before. He probably had tossed and turned as he struggled within himself. His loving wife, Sarah, always present, watches Abraham as he ponders the heavy burdens he is carrying. She has gone with him from Ur of the Chaldeans, their own home. She has been taken by Pharaoh into his harem. She has posed as his sister down in Egypt. At the age of ninety, Sarah is blessed of God and gives birth to Isaac. But never in her long life had she awakened to a morning like this one. She sits still in the tent. She does not ask any

questions. Abraham and Sarah watch as the two servants load the wood, and she unsuccessfully tries to
hold back her tears. With all the provisions now made
for the long journey, Abraham sends the promised boy,
Isaac, to say good-by to his mother. As far as Abraham
knows it is the last time that Isaac will ever see his
mother. For Isaac there is great anticipation and
excitement. He is going to take a trip with his father,
and he has never been to where they are going. But for
Sarah, a mother, there are tragic feelings.

Finally Abraham turns and looks at her as a husband learns to look at his wife after they have been
married for many years. Not a word spoken, they communicate. He takes her in his great, old wrinkled hands
and presses her face against his beard, and with tears
streaming down his face, he turns away from her and
looks into the new morning. Sarah watches as Abraham, Isaac, and the servants leave over the horizon.

For Abraham, Isaac, and the servants, the journey is
three days. All during the three days and nights of the
trip the words of God keep coming up in his mind:

> "Take now your son, your only son, whom you
> love, Isaac, and go to the land of Moriah; and offer
> him there as a burnt offering on one of the moun-
> tains of which I will tell you" (22:2).

Surely Abraham must have struggled with the idea:
"God, isn't there something else in my camp that I can
give You that would show You that I really do believe in
Your faithfulness? As I undergo the most severe test of
my faith in You, couldn't I have given you a herd of my
camels? Couldn't I have given you some of the trea-
sures of Egypt that were given to me?" The words of
God continued over in the mind of Abraham. Isaac,
who is his treasure, must now be sacrificed. But Abraham had continued to claim that God had called him.
After all, at seventy-five Abraham claimed that God
had called him to leave to go into Canaan. At ninety-

seven Abraham claimed that God reaffirmed His promises to him. At one hundred Abraham claimed that God
was especially with him when he was able to bring a
son into the world. In a pagan world that worshiped
water, air, dirt, and fire, Abraham and his family had
gotten hold of the idea of "God." Abraham worshiped
God, and as never before God is now testing the faith of
the great old man. As Abraham reached inside his
robes, he pulled out the dagger and lifted it high above
his head, and he must have looked down into the terri-
fied face of his own son, Isaac. Suddenly he hears the
words of God:

> "Abraham, Abraham!" ... "Do not stretch out your
> hand against the lad, and do nothing to him; for
> now I know that you fear God, since you have not
> withheld your son, your only son, from Me" (22:11,
> 12).

Abraham looks, and God has provided a sacrifice. A
ram is caught in some bushes that are nearby, and he
unties his promised son. He takes the wood off the boy's
back. Tears of joy flow down the old man's face as he
hugs his son. Then he runs down the side of Mount
Moriah and hurries home. What a great celebration
there must have been as he tells Sarah, with his heart
overflowing with joy, "I told you so. You can depend
upon Him. He is always faithful. He promised us that
through this son the descendants of the world would be
blessed." There must have been an overwhelming celebration in the tents of Abraham as he returns home to
celebrate the great God whom he has learned is faithful.

Why is this story in the Bible? What is it saying to
people who are trying to live the Christian life? Three
lessons come from this chapter.

The first lesson is the meaning of God's faithfuness.
Righteous living means doing the will of God (James
2:18). Nowhere does God promise us that when we are
living faithfully for Him that He will not test us. In fact

James says in chapter 1 that you ought to "count it joy" when your faith *is tested*. You know you are in the lineage of Abraham when your faith is tested. Mount Moriah is a place where pagans took their children and sacrificed them. Asking Abraham, as a non-pagan, as a believer in God, to go do something that pagans do makes absolutely no sense at all. And that is the very point! You and I will find ourselves in situations when life makes absolutely no sense whatsoever to us. It is not logical. It has no human logic to it whatsoever. God has promised and now given Isaac to Abraham, and He then says, "It is through this son that the descendants of you will be numerous and all the earth is to be blessed. Now go kill him!" That does not make sense. What do you do when you are faced with life and the problems of life make no sense to you? You do what Abraham did. You do not try to make sense out of it. You depend on the faithfulness of God. Abraham knew that even if the dagger went through the heart of Isaac—God would resurrect him (Hebrews 11). His dependence was in the faithfulness of God.

Second, for Abraham, Isaac was his special treasure. God tests Abraham by saying, "Be willing to sacrifice your treasure to Me." Is God interested in taking the life of a boy? Of course not! That is not the point of the story. What is the point? What is your Isaac? Is it your job? Has your work and making money become your Isaac? What is it that you hope for, dream about, and plan on? What is your greatest ambition? What is it you look to that commands respect in your life and makes impressions on people? Whatever it is, that is your Isaac, God would resurrect him (Hebrews 11). His dependence was in the faithfulness of God.

The third lesson involves the meaning of joy. What is the difference in a boring, guilt-ridden, non-evangelistic, non-celebrative, negative life and a forgiven, exciting, positive, evangelistic life? In the case of Abraham, the difference is the difference of joy. Abraham has

great joy because he has a personal relationship with
God. He has built his life on a personal relationship
with God, the Father. He trusts in God and in the faithfulness of God. We will never know the joy of Abraham
if we live on propositions instead of a relationship with
God. Rules never take the place of relationship. The
difference today in so many churches that are critical,
narrow-minded, ugly-spirited, and selfish compared to
churches that are generous and giving, compassionate,
on fire, growing, and evangelistic is the joy and having
no joy. When you have a relationship with God, you
experience overwhelming joy even as Abraham did
when he returned home to Sarah.

THE DEATH (23)

> Now Sarah lived one hundred and twenty-seven
> years; . . . (23:1).

We do not know how old Sarah was at her marriage.
We know that she was ninety when Isaac was born
(17:17). We can assume that it is many years later,
perhaps even many years after the test of Abraham
and Sarah's great faith (22). She died. Is the Bible not a
brilliant book inspired of God! It just tells the most
momentous events in the shortest language. She died.

> And Sarah died in Kiriath-arba (that is, Hebron) in
> the land of Canaan; and Abraham went in to
> mourn for Sarah and to weep for her (23:2).

The greatest gift that was ever given to Abraham was
Sarah. The greatest gift that is ever given to a Christian man is a Christian wife. How many times after she
died did he reach over to touch her, but she was not
there? How many times during the night did he struggle with grief and fear, but she was not there? Through
the entire marriage she followed Abraham. Jim
McGuiggan puts it this way in his book on Genesis,
"Then came rest, no more wandering, the end of a

sojourn. *And her husband followed her!"*[1]

> Then Abraham rose from before his dead, and
> spoke to the sons of Heth, saying, "I am a stranger
> and a sojourner among you; give me a burial site
> among you, that I may bury my dead out of my
> sight" (23:3, 4).

Abraham is not legally a citizen of the land on which he
is now walking. He requests a place for her burial.

> And the sons of Heth answered Abraham, saying
> to him, "Hear us, my lord, you are a mighty prince
> among us; bury your dead in the choicest of our
> graves; none of us will refuse you his grave for
> burying your dead" (23:5, 6).

They do not know God's plan at all, but they offer their
own cemetery. Something else is at work here. It is the
same thing that was at work in the previous chapter. It
is the faithfulness of God. The Hittites do not know
anything about it. Maybe Abraham does not know and
fully understand what is happening now, but watch the
faithfulness of God unfold in this event. God uses the
customs of the people of the Hittites. There is the
intercession.

> And he spoke with them, saying, "If it is your wish
> for me to bury my dead out of my sight, hear me,
> and approach Ephron the son of Zohar for me"
> (23:8).

The oriental custom is for citizens of the land to bargain with an alien on the ownership.

> "That he may give me the cave of Machpelah
> which he owns, which is at the end of his field; for
> the full price let him give it to me in your presence
> for a burial site" (23:9).

They bargain, "We will give you a grave. We will loan
you one of ours. You cannot own the land." Abraham

---

[1]Jim McGuiggan, *Genesis and Us* (Lubbock, Tex.: International
Biblical Resources, 1988), 166.

keeps saying, "Sell me the land. I'll pay for the land. I want to pay you, but I do not want it loaned to me. I want to buy it from the owner, Ephron." The next passage (23:10-13) tells how Abraham buys according to the ancient custom. He buys the cave for four hundred shekels of silver. He does it in public. He is the owner.

> And after this, Abraham buried Sarah his wife in the cave of the field at Machpelah facing Mamre (that is, Hebron) in the land of Canaan (23:19).

So what does God do even through the death of Sarah? He begins the fulfillment of His great land He promised to Abraham. It is not loaned. It is not on credit. Abraham owns it. It is the cave of Machpelah, and God plans it in the land of Canaan. Years later when the Israelites go into the land of Canaan—guess what is awaiting them? The cave! The most famous burial spot in all of the Old Testament. Remember those buried in it: Sarah, Abraham, Isaac, Rebekah, Jacob, and Leah— the three great patriarchs and their wives in whom God has been working His promises. Great is the faithfulness of God. As Israel comes years later into Canaan, waiting those great Israelites in the land promised by God is land already owned by Israel—the cave of Machpelah.

THE JOY (24)

When Isaac marries Rebekah, it is a moment of joy.

> Now Abraham was old, advanced in age; and the Lord had blessed Abraham in every way (24:1).

Custom now demands that Abraham arrange the marriage of his son, Isaac. Through this child the descendants will be blessed and the land taken. The servant makes an oath to Abraham. The oath has two important conditions: (1) He is not to get a wife from the Canaanites and (2) he is to get a wife from the family.

> And Abraham said to his servant, the oldest of his
> household, who had charge of all that he owned,
> "Please place your hand under my thigh, and I will
> make you swear by the Lord, the God of heaven
> and the God of earth, that you shall not take a wife
> for my son from the daughters of the Canaanites,
> among whom I live, but you shall go to my country
> and to my relatives, and take a wife for my son
> Isaac." And the servant said to him, "Suppose the
> woman will not be willing to follow me to this land;
> should I take your son back to the land from where
> you came?" (24:2-5).

Abraham says no, "No, do not do that":

> Then Abraham said to him, "Beware lest you take
> my son back there!" (24:6).

Why? Because Abraham knows what marriage can be.
Abraham knows that a young man can easily be physically attracted to a young woman. The young woman
can easily be physically and emotionally attracted to
the young man. Isaac is a believer in God, the God of
Abraham and Sarah. But the woman may be a worshiper of the Canaanite gods. Abraham reasons, "If
she refuses to come, you are relieved of the conditions of
the oath." So, the servant begins the process of praying
to God. God is in control of the choice of Isaac's wife.
She must not hinder Isaac from his deep commitment
to God and to His purposes.

> And he said, "O Lord, the God of my master Abra-
> ham, please grant me success today, and show
> lovingkindness to my master Abraham. Behold, I
> am standing by the spring, and the daughters of
> the men of the city are coming out to draw water;
> now may it be that the girl to whom I say, 'Please
> let down your jar so that I may drink,' and who
> answers, 'Drink, and I will water your camels
> also';—may she be the one whom Thou hast ap-
> pointed for Thy servant Isaac; and by this I shall
> know that Thou hast shown lovingkindness to my
> master" (24:12-14).

There is a wonderful lesson here: Before marriage, we
need to go to God and ask God to make the selection of
our marriage partner. Marriage is so crucial. It is the
second most vital relationship. It is second only to one's
relationship to God and Jesus Christ. This servant,
knowing the mind of Abraham, prayed to God that He
would select Isaac's wife. The story continues as Rebekah comes out just as he is ending the prayer:

> Then the servant ran to meet her, and said, "Please
> let me drink a little water from your jar." And she
> said, "Drink, my lord"; and she quickly lowered
> her jar to her hand, and gave him a drink. Now
> when she had finished giving him a drink, she
> said, "I will draw also for your camels until they
> have finished drinking" (24:17-19).

The servant knows it is this woman by the name of
Rebekah. The negotiations continue through the older
brother as according to custom. The servant meets with
Rebekah's family and fulfills all of Abraham's require-
ments. Gifts are exchanged. The servant then states
his mission to the family. He states it in such a way that
God is a part of it. Rebekah's father and brothers place
clear confidence in the faithfulness of God.

> Thus they sent away their sister Rebekah and her
> nurse with Abraham's servant and his men. And
> they blessed Rebekah and said to her, "May you,
> our sister, become thousands of ten thousands,
> and may your descendants possess the gate of
> those who hate them" (24:59, 60).

Isaac sees Rebekah and the servant coming and
rushes out to meet her. She becomes his wife, and he
loves her. There is great, great joy in the family now.
What a magnificent theme—God's faithfulness. "Take
your son and sacrifice him. I'm in control. Bury your
wife in this cave. Buy the cave. I want the cave in the
family because later I will guide the nation back to the
land. Select a wife. If you will pray to Me, I am faithful,

and I will select the proper wife for Isaac. Her name will be Rebekah." The faithfulness of God from the great book of Genesis! Depend on Him. "Great is Thy faithfulness"!

QUESTIONS

1. What trial did God give Abraham and Sarah?

2. Why would He ask for such a thing?

3. What three lessons come from chapter 22?

4. How does God use the death of Sarah?

5. What does the marriage of Isaac to Rebekah tell us in terms of our selection of a marriage partner?

11 Genesis 25—27

Making Peace With Your Shadow

One person describes himself as "a walking civil war." It is the same inner conflict that a man felt when he had the following sign directed at the McNeil Island Federal Prison: "I have had more trouble with John Smith than any man I know. Signed, John Smith." Any serious introspection will surface the enemy we carry within ourselves. Paul understood very well this conflict and confessed it in his familiar statement: "I don't do the good I want to do; instead, I do the evil that I do not want to do. . . . So I find that this law is at work: when I want to do what is good, what is evil is the only choice I have" (Romans 7:19, 21; TEV).

How do we bring harmony out of the civil war of inner conflict? The only route to take is total honesty with God. The more transparent we are with God, the less we need to play games with Him and others. Carl Jung called the adversary within each of us "the shadow" of each of us. Until we become transparent, we may try to hide this shadow so that we can be attractive to others. John Powell says that the reason that we do not tell others who we *really* are is due to our fear of rejection. We cannot become whole persons until we learn to reconcile the two people we are.

Stan Mooneyham in *Dancing on the Strait and Narrow* describes the transformation of one's personality into a more creative, honest, and dedicated Christian in the following way:

> Or to put it another way, it means kissing the frog so he may become a prince. Do you remember the fable? Good looking but vain and mean, the prince showed few character traits that befit his noble birth. A witch turned him into a frog, giving him a physical appearance to match his personality. The curse could be lifted only when the frog was kissed by a princess who would love and accept the creature as he really was.[1]

Mooneyham calls this spiritual transformation "making peace with your shadow."

JACOB'S BIRTH AND DECEPTION (25:19-34)

> Now these are the records of the generations of Isaac, Abraham's son; . . . (25:19).

This important phrase occurs several times in Genesis. Some scholars believe that such a reference seems to be a heading for a new section of Scripture and may denote the various tablets which Moses used to write Genesis. Divine inspiration does not eliminate the idea of sources. For example, we know that Luke used sources to write his Gospel.

> Isaac was forty years old when he took Rebekah, the daughter of Bethuel the Aramean of Paddan-aram, the sister of Laban the Aramean, to be his wife (25:20).

Jacob came from revered stock. Abraham is Jacob's grandfather, and Isaac and Rebekah are Jacob's par-

---

[1]Stan Mooneyham, *Dancing on the Strait and Narrow* (San Francisco: Harper & Row, 1989), 98.

ents. One of the best things Isaac ever did was to marry Rebekah. Even though he may have been a fairly average person, she appears in Scripture to be creative, imaginative, gifted, and very strong. Grief, however, filled her life because she failed in the only way that women of antiquity believed they could fulfill themselves. She could not have children.

> And Isaac prayed to the Lord on behalf of his wife, because she was barren; and the Lord answered him and Rebekah his wife conceived (25:21).

Sometimes we pray about a matter and give up after a few prayers. Isaac prayed for twenty years! Isaac knows that by faithfully praying he can believe that God will fulfill His promise though it may take many yeas. In fact, people of faith may never see the fulfillment of God's promises while living on earth (Hebrews 11:39).

> But the children struggled together within her; ... (25:22).

Rebekah thinks this continuous struggle in her womb is crucial enough that she consults God. God says,

> "Two nations are in your womb; and two peoples shall be separated from your body; and one people shall be stronger than the other; and the older shall serve the younger" (25:23).

The rivalry between Jacob (later known as Israel) and Esau (later known as Edom) begins at their birth. The first child to be born had skin "like a hairy garment," so he was named Esau. Right behind him is a second son with his hand on the heel of the first as if he is tripping him. It is a sign of future events, and the second son is given the appropriate name of Jacob, "heel grabber."

Esau becomes an outdoorsman, a hunter, and his father's favorite son. Jacob becomes a devious con man, deceitful, and his mother's favorite. An interesting story of deception unfolds.

> And when Jacob had cooked stew, Esau came in
> from the field and he was famished (25:29).

Esau comes in from a day of hunting and smells the
aroma of Jacob's stew. Famished and unwilling to wait
until dinner is ready, Esau's impulsiveness gets the
best of him.

> Esau said to Jacob, "Please let me have a swallow
> of that red stuff there, for I am famished" (25:30).

Some scholars translate this, "Let me gulp that red."
Hebrews 12:16, 17 says Esau was sexually "immoral"
and "godless" (not given to spiritual concerns), so his
next move could be anticipated.

> But Jacob said, "First sell me your birthright"
> (25:31).

The birthright stands for the headship of the family
and a double share of the estate. Included in this birthright are two additional things in the inheritance: the
promised land and the promised seed. Only a spiritually discerning mind would have special interests in
this birthright.

> And Esau said, "Behold, I am about to die; so of
> what use then is the birthright to me?" . . . Thus
> Esau despised his birthright (25:32-34).

Esau lives for momentary satisfaction and gives up the
eternal and the important. He decides to refuse everything God has for him and makes a tragic decision. On
the other hand, Jacob has a more discerning spirit and
sees the spiritual value of the birthright. Though deceptive, Jacob gets on the frequency of God. In short, this is
one of the costliest meals ever served. Esau lost his
future, though he probably thought he lost nothing. For
a momentary experience of satisfaction, Esau turns his
back on the plans that God has for his life. It is so easy
to condemn Esau at this point in the story. But how
often are we tempted to eat, drink, and sell out every-

thing God has for us? What is the difference between Jacob and Esau? Though Jacob deceives his brother, his heart really seeks God's will for his life. He is hungry and thirsty for spiritual things while Esau loves stew.

LIKE FATHER, LIKE SON (26)

Notice that the emphasis of this chapter is not on Jacob, but his father, Isaac. Chapter 27 will shift back to Jacob. Recall that chapters 25 through 37 are the history of Jacob including the important events in his spiritual development. Chapter 26 is not a detour into the irrelevant. It is the story of members of his family which allows us to understand more fully the life of Jacob.

> Now there was a famine in the land, . . . (26:1).

Genesis will frequently mention famine as a test of the patriarch's faith. It was a famine which caused Abraham to leave the land of Canaan and go down into Egypt. Another famine now causes Isaac to also travel toward Egypt. In a spiritual sense, any barren, dry, and unproductive moment when God does not seem close can be properly called "a famine." Like Abraham and Isaac, we also go through these moments, and they try our reliance on God.

> The Lord appeared to him and said, "Do not go down to Egypt; stay in the land of which I shall tell you. Sojourn in this land and I will be with you and bless you, . . . I will multiply your descendants as the stars of heaven, . . . and by your descendants all the nations of the earth shall be blessed; . . ." (26:2-5).

This is the first time that Genesis records God speaking directly to Isaac. Isaac's faith in God probably comes from the example of faith he saw in Abraham. Now God speaks directly to Isaac and confirms the covenant which He made with Abraham. Unlike Abraham who went down into Egypt, Isaac obeys God and stays in Gerar. For Isaac, Gerar has the memories of childhood. Here is where Abraham dug wells, where Isaac grew up, and where the Philistines respected Isaac's family.

> When the men of the place asked about his wife, he said, "She is my sister," . . . (26:7-11).

Isaac seems to forget that God is providing special and personal care for him. He deceives Abimelech and his men. Isaac lies about Rebekah out of fear that he will be killed and she will be taken. His fear surpasses his faith in the divine promise that God would be with him and build a great nation from his descendants. Where did Isaac learn to lie like this? From Abraham, his father. Children almost always deal with their problems in the same way that their parents meet their problems. This is a powerful example of the influence of parents and the way in which children imitate their own parents.

> . . . Abimelech king of the Philistines looked out through a window, and saw, and behold, Isaac was caressing his wife Rebekah (26:8).

When Abimelech looks through a window and watches Isaac, he sees Isaac caressing Rebekah. Some scholars believe that the word translated "caressing" is based on Isaac's name. If so, Isaac may have been causing his wife to laugh.

> So Abimelech charged all the people, saying, "He who touches this man or his wife shall surely be put to death" (26:11).

How strange that a pagan king holds to a tighter moral code than a believer in God! Abimelech rebukes Isaac and prohibits any man from taking Isaac's wife because it would be adultery. Genesis clearly reveals city-states which have laws protecting family relationships and prohibiting adultery. It is inaccurate to think of Israel as a tower of moral strength surrounded by immoral nations who know nothing of God or of His life. True, many of the people of Canaan rejected God's way, but several of the nations who have contact with Israel demonstrate a higher sense of morality than the ancient patriarchs. As Paul will later claim in Romans 1, God's truth has become available to all men everywhere. Abimelech has a high sense of morality and chastises Isaac for his lack of faith and moral courage.

> Now Isaac sowed in that land, and reaped in the same year a hundredfold. And the Lord blessed him, . . . (26:12-35).

Isaac reopens wells to which he has rights through treaties between Abraham and Abimelech. No doubt, Isaac has a title to these wells and the surrounding lands. While these wells are his by right, he chooses not to claim them by his rights. When the herdsmen of Gerar quarrel with Isaac's herdsmen, he abandons the well and calls it "Esek," meaning "dispute, contention" (26:20). A second well is contended, and Isaac calls it "Sitnah," meaning "adversity" (26:21). He moves about twenty miles away from Gerar and names his new well "Rehoboth," meaning "wide spaces" (26:22). He names his last well "Shibah," meaning "oath" (26:33). Isaac could have fought for rights, for he had every legal argument on his side. Instead, he follows the direction of God and allows God to take care of his problem.

> And they brought grief to Isaac and Rebekah (26:35).

Esau's godless marriages break his parents' hearts. Not really concerned with faith and spiritual matters, Esau marries unbelievers. Such marriages became a major source of family pain to believing parents.

EACH IN JACOB'S FAMILY HAS A SHADOW (27)

It is often tempting to elevate patriarchs above where the Bible really places them. We see the faith of Abraham and forget how he deceived others. Genesis records the humanity, the shadowy side of each of the members of Jacob's family. In the following story, Isaac seems spiritually unaware, Rebekah is manipulating for her own interests, Esau is spiritually impulsive, and Jacob is deceptive. One can take consolation from this story by realizing all of the above are used by God to develop His mysterious providential plan in ancient history.

> Now it came about, when Isaac was old, and his eyes were too dim to see, that he called his older son Esau.... (27:1).

Isaac is a man of great trust in God; he is the product of Abraham. But now we see how he yields his faith to the pressure of doing things his own way. He calls Esau to him and tries to manipulate his favorite son into a situation so he may bless Esau, whom he deeply loves.

> And Isaac said, "... prepare a savory dish for me such as I love, ... so that my soul may bless you before I die" (27:2-4).

Isaac tells Esau to go hunting and to prepare his favorite stew as a special moment for receiving his father's blessing.

> And Rebekah was listening while Isaac spoke to his son Esau.... (27:5-17).

Somebody overhears Isaac's instructions to Esau. The somebody is Rebekah. And she has her favorite son too. She devises a plan which includes preparing a special meat dish for blind Isaac and dressing Jacob in Esau's clothes. The goatskins will make Isaac think that he is blessing Esau, the hairy one. Jacob begins a long series of deceptions: "I am Esau your first-born."

Next he says, "I have done as you told me." Then he says, "Eat of my game, that you may bless me." Even though he is old and blind, Isaac is skeptical because of Jacob's voice, but he feels the goatskin and smells Esau's clothes. Rebekah and Jacob have totally deceived Isaac.

> ... he blessed him and said, "... may God give you of the dew of heaven, and of the fatness of the earth, ... May peoples serve you, and nations bow down to you; ..." (27:27-29).

Isaac gives Jacob the land, the great seed promise, and domination over his brother. Ancient blessings such as this one were final, unrepeatable, and definite. Ancient records indicate that such blessings would stand up in a court of law and could not be overturned for any reason.

> Now it came about, as soon as Isaac had finished blessing Jacob, and Jacob had hardly gone out from the presence of Isaac his father, that Esau his brother came in from his hunting. . . . (27:30-40).

What a marvelous story! Just as Jacob leaves in the nick of time, Esau comes in to Isaac's tent as if on cue. He brings his own stew and is ready to receive his father's blessing. In Hebrews 12:17, Esau seeks his favor and tries to get Isaac to change his mind, but Isaac cannot. The only blessing Isaac has for Esau is the bleak future of living around the Dead Sea, living by the sword, and being dominated by his brother.

> So Esau bore a grudge against Jacob because of the blessing with which his father had blessed him; . . . (27:41-46).

Knowing that Esau will kill her favorite son, Rebekah again uses her imagination and sends Jacob away to marry in her family. Jacob leaves home in fear and runs away from his problem. Rebekah will never again see him. Jacob will later have to face his own shadow and learn to make peace with it, but that is another part of the story.

QUESTIONS

1. Why is it important to "make peace with your shadow"?

2. What does "Jacob" mean, and what does it symbolize?

3. In what sense is Jacob like his father?

4. According to Paul, what does the case of Jacob and Esau tell us about God (Romans 9:10-16)?

5. How does each member of Jacob's family have its own shadow?

Jacob:
The Crippling
Crisis

A turning point in someone's life can mean the loss of a job, an automobile accident, an illness, or a family crisis. These raise some deep and searching questions about the future, about faith, about God. In all of these instances, the term "turning point" means a crossroads, a crisis, a moment of opportunity but also a moment in which there could be some very serious tragedy.

JACOB MEETS GOD (28)

Genesis 28 is the beginning of one of the major crises, crossroads, or turning points in the life of Jacob.

> So Isaac called Jacob and blessed him and charged him, and said to him, "You shall not take a wife from the daughters of Canaan. Arise, go to Paddan-aram, to the house of Bethuel your mother's father; and from there take to yourself a wife from the daughters of Laban your mother's brother" (28:1, 2).

Jacob leaves for a 450-mile trip. He leaves to go toward the Euphrates River so he can marry someone in his faith. He will marry a daughter of his Uncle Laban.

God directs Jacob to marry someone in the faith. We see this issue arise again and again. As Jacob begins to move closer and closer to the will of God, notice that his brother Esau moves spiritually further and further from the will of God. Already Esau has married a Hittite or maybe several Hittite women. At this point you will notice the Word of God says:

> So Esau saw that the daughters of Canaan displeased his father Isaac; and Esau went to Ishmael, and married, besides the wives that he had, Mahalath the daughter of Ishmael, Abraham's son, the sister of Nebaioth (28:8, 9).

He marries someone who is outside the messianic line. At times we as human beings may question God. We may question His right of sovereignty. We may wonder if God is mapping out the life of Jacob in such a way that Jacob cannot make any choices. Is He pulling the strings on the life of Esau in such a way that Esau cannot make any choices? Here is a case in point that shows us the exact opposite is true. Jacob is making some decisions that are in accord or in alignment with the will of God. Esau, on the other hand, is a person who is moving away from the heart of God. He has already married one, or more, women who are not in his faith; they are Hittites. They do not worship God. There is not anything about their religion that is close to the worship of God. And now, Esau decides, "I'll not only do that, but because of the resentment that I still have, I am going to marry someone else that is outside the messianic line." He marries an Ishmaelite, and her name is Mahalath.

We are about to see the first appearance of God to Jacob. He appeared to Abraham several times. He appeared to Isaac only once, as recorded in Genesis. He appears to Jacob seven times. This is a turning point in the life of Jacob. Jacob must be at least seventy years of age. He has spent most of his life at home. He leaves

Beersheba, the southern part of the land of Canaan. He is on his way toward Mesopotamia, a 450-mile northest journey to the Euphrates River.

> Then Jacob departed from Beersheba and went toward Haran. And he came to a certain place and spent the night there, because the sun had set; and he took one of the stones of the place and put it under his head, and lay down in that place (28:10, 11).

The city was known as Luz. When Jacob gets there, the city has been destroyed and there is nothing left but stones. No people are living there. He takes one of the stones, using it as a pillow, and falls asleep. He is lonely and frightened. He probably has built a fire to cook some food, and as the embers of the fire are fading away, he begins to sleep.

> And he had a dream, and behold, a ladder was set on the earth with its top reching to heaven; and behold, the angels of God were ascending and descending on it (28:12).

We cannot see angels, but the Word of God describes them as the messengers of God. An angel of God announces the birth of Jesus. Angels are sent to guard over us. An angel of God will blow the trumpet announcing the second coming of Jesus Christ. And so Jacob dreams that angels are going to God and that angels are going from God to him. What a beautiful dream. Here God is saying in effect, "I will take care of you. You have access to Me, and I have access to you. I will guard you. I know you are alone. I know you have a 450-mile journey, but you are doing My will. I don't want you to marry outside the faith. I don't want you to marry a Hittite or a Canaanite woman. They do not worship Me. You align yourself with Me, and I will care for you. You will always have access to Me."

And behold, the Lord stood above it and said, "I

am the Lord, the God of your father Abraham and the God of Isaac; the land on which you lie, I will give it to you and to your descendants. [This is the land promise.] Your descendants shall also be like the dust of the earth, and you shall spread out to the west and to the east and to the north and to the south; and in you and in your descendants shall all the families of the earth be blessed. [This is the great nation promise. Next is the great presence promise.] And behold, I am with you, and will keep you wherever you go, and will bring you back to this land; for I will not leave you until I have done what I have promised you." Then Jacob awoke from his sleep and said, "Surely the Lord is in this place, and I did not know it." And he was afraid and said, "How awesome is this place! This is none other than the house of God, and this is the gate of heaven."

So Jacob rose early in the morning, and took the stone that he had put under his head and set it up as a pillar, and poured oil on its top. And he called the name of that place Bethel; however, previously the name of the city had been Luz. [Bethel means "house of God." It used to be an old Canaanite city, Luz, but now it has a new name.] Then Jacob made a vow, saying, "If God will be with me and will keep me on this journey that I take, and will give me food to eat and garments to wear, and I return to my father's house in safety, then the Lord will be my God. And this stone, which I have set up as a pillar, will be God's house; and of all that Thou dost give me I will surely give a tenth to Thee" (28:13-22).

Jacob has a great moment with God in which God tells him He would be with Jacob. Jacob then covenants with God and tells Him he will be His servant and will give a tenth.

JACOB MARRIES RACHEL (29:1-30)

Jacob marries a woman in the faith. This is the plan of God, the will of God. He travels to "the land of the sons of the east." This phrase refers to the area around

Mesopotamia, the Fertile Crescent, the Tigris and Euphrates Rivers. It is here he sees a well in the field and flocks around it. A large stone rests over the mouth of the well. The shepherds would remove the stone so they could water their sheep.

> While he was still speaking with them, Rachel came with her father's sheep, for she was a shepherdess. And it came about, when Jacob saw Rachel the daughter of Laban his mother's brother, and the sheep of Laban his mother's brother, that Jacob went up, and rolled the stone from the mouth of the well, and watered the flock of Laban his mother's brother. Then Jacob kissed Rachel, and lifted his voice and wept. And Jacob told Rachel that he was a relative of her father and that he was Rebekah's son, and she ran and told her father (29:9-12).

They have never seen each other, apparently. Though they have lived five hundred miles from one another, he has come to marry a woman of his faith. Laban hears the good news about Jacob. He embraces him, welcomes him with the kiss, brings him into his home, and says, "Surely you are my bone and my flesh" (29:14).

Jacob works seven years in an agreement with Laban for Rachel. At the end of those seven years, he is deceived by Laban and is given the older of the two daughters, according to the custom in Mesopotamia. Her name is Leah. She is not nearly as beautiful as Rachel. She is described as having weak eyes (perhaps cross-eyed). But Jacob was in love with Rachel and said he would work another seven years in return for her.

JACOB'S FAMILY (29:31—30:43)

Leah has four sons: Reuben, Simeon, Levi, and Judah. Bilhah has two sons by Jacob: Dan and Naphtali. Zilpah has two sons by the names of Gad and Asher. Leah has two more sons, Issachar and Zebulun. She then has a daughter whose name is Dinah.

Rachel, who has been barren all of these years, has attempted on her own initiative with Leah and with these maidservants to make the will of God come true. God remembers Rachel and opens her womb. She gives birth to a son, and his name is Joseph (30:22-24).

Laban and Jacob begin to outsmart one another (30:25-43). There is the bargain for the severance pay as Jacob decides now that he wants to go back home to his land. He now has children. He has Rachel, whom he loves a great deal, and Leah, whom he does not love as much. He bargains with Laban, "Let me go, and the bargain that I will make is that I will go to your herds and pull the speckled ones and the dark ones away as mine." Laban agrees, but he takes all the dark ones out one night and places them in the care of his sons. Why is Laban deceiving Jacob? "Whatever a man sows, that shall he also reap." Jacob has deceived everyone in his past. Even his name means "being deceitful," literally "grabbing the heel." Jacob sowed the seed; Laban is simply letting him harvest some of that deceit.

Jacob tricks Laban. He does so by mating all of the sheep together so that they will become spotted or dark. It is very difficult to out trick or to out think Jacob. Deceit is second nature to him.

HOUSEHOLD GODS (31)

Jacob plans to leave. He sends word to Rachel and Leah, and they come out to the fields. They get all the children, the servants, and the flocks together, and they leave secretly from the land of Mesopotamia (Aramea as it is also called). They start that trip back down toward the southern Negev, down toward the great promised land.

Laban pursues Jacob. At this point we do not know why Laban is pursuing Jacob. But why does he assemble this large entourage of family members and go this long distance to pursue them?

> "And now you have indeed gone away because you
> longed greatly for your father's house; but why did
> you steal my gods?" Then Jacob answered and
> said to Laban, "Because I was afraid, for I said,
> 'Lest you would take your daughters from me by
> force.' The one with whom you find your gods shall
> not live; in the presence of our kinsmen point out
> what is yours among my belongings and take it for
> yourself." For Jacob did not know that Rachel had
> stolen them (31:30-32).

According to ancient mythology, if you do not have
your god with you, then you could be in great trouble. If
you do not have your god with you, you do not know
how to worship him. He may strike you and your family
with illness, a financial crisis, or a personal crisis.
When Laban discovers that the entourage had not only
left to return home, but that they had also taken the
family gods, he starts pursuing them. Jacob does not
know the gods have been stolen. He does not know that
when Rachel left home, she thought not only would she
need the living God, but she might also need some of
these Canaanite gods.

> So Laban went into Jacob's tent, and into Leah's
> tent, and into the tent of the two maids, but he did
> not find them. Then he went out of Leah's tent and
> entered Rachel's tent. Now Rachel had taken the
> household idols and put them in the camel's sad-
> dle, and she sat on them. And Laban felt through
> all the tent, but did not find them. And she said to
> her father, "Let not my lord be angry that I cannot
> rise before you, for the manner of women is upon
> me." So he searched, but did not find the household
> idols.
> Then Jacob became angry and contended with
> Laban; and Jacob answered and said to Laban,
> "What is my transgression? What is my sin, that
> you have hotly pursued me? Though you have felt
> through all my goods, what have you found of all
> your household goods? Set it here before my kins-
> men and your kinsmen, that they may decide
> between us two" (31:33-37).

Laban had not found the idols at this point. It is a miscarriage of justice as far as Jacob is concerned. They complain that Rachel has stolen them.

Laban and Jacob make a covenant together. They seal the covenant and call the place Mizpah, "May the Lord watch between you and me when we are absent one from the other" (31:49). Laban goes back to Mesopotamia, to his family.

> And early in the morning Laban arose, and kissed his sons and his daughters and blessed them. Then Laban departed and returned to his place (31:55).

GOD MEETS JACOB (32)

We begin to prepare for the second turning point in the life of Jacob. He prepares to meet his brother, Esau. He must meet and deal with Esau in order to get back where he needs to be. He deceived Esau out of his birthright and blessing. Esau has been extremely angry and is called in the New Testament "a godless man."

Jacob, in preparation to meet his brother, Esau, sends messengers to go ahead, and they are to tell Esau:

> "I have oxen and donkeys and flocks and male and female servants; and I have sent to tell my lord, that I may find favor in your sight." And the messengers returned to Jacob, saying, "We came to your brother Esau, and furthermore he is coming to meet you, and four hundred men are with him" (32:5, 6).

Esau has an army of four hundred men. It is not a "party" group to welcome Jacob back home across the river. This scares Jacob to death. He sees what his deceit has led him to face.

> Then Jacob was greatly afraid and distressed; and he divided the people who were with him, and the flocks and the herds and the camels, into two companies; for he said, "If Esau comes to the one com-

pany and attacks it, then the company which is
left will escape" (32:7, 8).

He gives instructions on how they are to give gifts and
how they are to meet Esau.

> So he spent the night there. Then he selected
> from what he had with him a present for his
> brother Esau: two hundred female goats and twen-
> ty male goats, two hundred ewes and twenty rams,
> thirty milking camels and their colts, forty cows
> and ten bulls, twenty female donkeys and ten male
> donkeys. And he delivered them into the hand of
> his servants, every drove by itself, and said to his
> servants, "Pass on before me, and put a space
> between droves." And he commanded the one in
> front, saying, "When my brother Esau meets you
> and asks you, saying, 'To whom do you belong,
> and where are you going, and to whom do these
> animals in front of you belong?' then you shall say,
> 'These belong to your servant Jacob; it is a present
> sent to my lord Esau. And behold, he also is behind
> us' " (32:13-18).

Jacob is a smart man: "Get the gifts out there in front.
Maybe when he sees all the animals and all the servants that I'm giving him, he will loosen up his resentment and anger and he won't kill me."

Now comes the second turning point in Jacob's life.
Jacob has been trusting in Jacob all of his life. He has
been a deceitful man. He has been a man who has
fought his own battles, but his heart has been aligned
toward God. Now comes the wrestling with God.

> Now he arose that same night and took his two
> wives and his two maids and his eleven children,
> and crossed the ford of the Jabbok. And he took
> them and sent them across the stream. And he sent
> across whatever he had. Then Jacob was left
> alone, and a man wrestled with him until day-
> break. And when he saw that he had not prevailed
> against him, he touched the socket of his thigh; so
> the socket of Jacob's thigh was dislocated while he
> wrestled with him. Then he said, "Let me go, for

the dawn is breaking." But he said, "I will not let you go unless you bless me." So he said to him, "What is your name?" And he said, "Jacob." And he said, "Your name shall no longer be Jacob, but Israel; for you have striven with God and with men and have prevailed." Then Jacob asked him and said, "Please tell me your name." But he said, "Why is it that you ask my name?" And he blessed him there. So Jacob named the place Peniel, for he said, "I have seen God face to face, yet my life has been preserved" (32:22-30).

God has to isolate Jacob before He can get Jacob's attention. There was no Rachel, no Leah, no herds, no bargaining power, no leverage, no money or possessions. Everything he has is on the other side of the Jabbok. God now has Jacob where He has been wanting to get him for years. Alone. Away from the preoccupations and distractions. Jacob then wrestles with the God/man. The ancients believed that if you could possess a god's name you could control him. Without the identity of a god, one has no way of using that god. But Jacob cannot control God. Jacob finally submits to God. God does not force Himself on Jacob. God says, "You will no longer be called a deceitful person 'Jacob'; you will be called 'Israel,' 'exalted one with God.' " Jacob now is a different person. Here is a man who has always been willing to deceive to get his own way. Even his name meant deceitful "heel-grabber." But now alone, with nothing to depend upon but God, he finally submits to God. He wrestles with God all night long and then submits to God. This is a great memorial to the weakness of Jacob.

Jacob limps the rest of his life. Every time he takes a step, he remembers that night, that turning point in his life when he wrestled with God all night long until the daylight, and finally submitted to God. When we wrestle with God, we are confronted with our inability to defeat Him. When we trust ourselves, we are weak. When we trust God, we are strong.

JACOB MEETS ESAU (33—35)

Chapter 33

Esau does not kill him. Esau kisses Jacob and embraces him. God is in this now. The children come, and Jacob finds favor in the sight of Esau.

Chapter 34

A horrible event now takes place. Dinah, Leah's daughter, goes out into one of the Hivite cities by herself, and Shechem rapes her. Shechem is obviously not a believer. He is not an Israelite. He is a man who sees this woman and is attracted to her physically: "And he was deeply attracted to Dinah. . . ." (v. 3). She appealed to him.

Jacob and his sons learn of the rape of Dinah. A marriage is quickly arranged.

> "And intermarry with us; give your daughters to us, and take our daughters for yourselves. Thus you shall live with us, and the land shall be open before you; live and trade in it, and acquire property in it" (34:9, 10).

These people who do not worship God are saying, "Marry our children, and we will marry your children." The plot is set (vv. 13-19) in which the brothers say, "We agree to this if all of the males in the city of Shechem will be circumcised." While the men are still in pain from the circumcision, they are murdered. Every male in the city of Shechem is killed. Simeon and Levi, the brothers of Dinah, go in and kill with their swords every man and every boy who has been circumcised. They seized everything in the city.

> And they captured and looted all their wealth and all their little ones and their wives, even all that was in the houses. Then Jacob said to Simeon and Levi, "You have brought trouble on me, by making me odious among the inhabitants of the land, among the Canaanites and the Perizzites; and my men being few in number, they will gather together

against me and attack me and I shall be destroyed,
I and my household." But they said, "Should he
treat our sister as a harlot?" (34:29-31).

Why would two men, brought up under Jacob, go
murder a whole city? Why would they steal their
women and children and take all of their possessions.
What is going on? We find out when we get to the next
chapter.

Chapter 35

Then God said to Jacob, "Arise, go up to Bethel,
and live there; and make an altar there to God, who
appeared to you when you fled from your brother
Esau" (35:1).

God has been telling Jacob to go to Bethel. He was
around all these people who do not believe in God. God
tells him again to go to Bethel and build an altar. Do
you not remember the two turning points in your life,
Jacob?

So Jacob said to his household and to all who were
with him, "Put away the foreign gods which are
among you, . . ." (35:2).

The ancient gods raped each other, murdered each
other, killed and plundered each other. While Jacob has
been struggling with faith, members of his own family
have been worshiping other gods. When Simeon and
Levi decide to get even at these people for their sister's
rape, they kill every man there. We always become like
what we worship. Jacob's family is falling apart right
in front of his eyes. He is worshiping God. We keep
wondering, Why does he not just get back home? What
is the problem? How in the world can you explain
murder, rape, and pillage? We can explain it easily
when we realize they are worshiping foreign gods. He
says to repent of idolatry.

"... purify yourselves, and change your garments;

and let us arise and go up to Bethel; and I will make an altar there to God, who answered me in the day of my distress, and has been with me wherever I have gone." So they gave to Jacob all the foreign gods which they had, and the rings which were in their ears; and Jacob hid them under the oak which was near Shechem (35:2-5).

Is that not beautiful? He does not put them in his saddlebags. He buries these gods at the roots of a tree. He leaves these gods at the foot of a tree in Shechem.

As they journeyed, there was a great terror upon the cities which were around them, and they did not pursue the sons of Jacob. . . . God also said to him, "I am God Almighty; be fruitful and multiply; a nation and a company of nations shall come from you, and kings shall come forth from you." . . . And Jacob set up a pillar in the place where He had spoken with him, a pillar of stone, and he poured out a libation on it; he also poured oil on it. So Jacob named the place where God had spoken with him, Bethel (35:5, 11, 14, 15).

This is a powerful lesson having to do with our faith and our families. So many times we rationalize that we can worship the gods of our culture and also worship God. We cannot sing, "O how I love Jesus," and then give our lives to serving materialism, success, and the other idols that are in our culture. Jacob's family just disintegrated right in front of his eyes. God wants us to be faithful to Him. He wants us to be at Bethel.

QUESTIONS

1. How does God interrupt or intersect the life of Jacob?

2. Some Bible scholars think Jacob's response to God (28:18-22) shows great faith and trust, while other scholars think Jacob has a twisted view of God.

What do you think and why?

3. How does Jacob's life illustrate that deception leads to deception?

4. What is the importance of the household gods to Jacob's family? Do certain sinful habits run in many families?

5. What is the significance of the change of name from "Jacob" to "Israel"?

13 Genesis 37—50

Overcoming Hardship

On a tomb in Springfield, Illinois, these words are engraved: "There lies the most perfect ruler of men the world has ever seen. Now, he belongs to the ages." Of whom was that said? Was it said of one of the great Roman Caesars? Was it said of Napoleon? Of what great man, described as "the most perfect ruler of men the world has ever seen," were those words spoken? Consider his life just for a moment.

At the age of 9, his mother died.

At 22, he got a job as a store clerk and then was fired.

At 23, he went into debt with another gentleman to buy a store. The other man was not good for his debt, and he had to pay off the entire indebtedness.

At 37, after three tries, he was elected to the U.S. Congress.

At 41, his four-year-old son died.

At 45, he ran for the U.S. Senate and lost.

At 47, he was defeated in his bid to become Vice President of the United States.

At 49, he ran for the U.S. Senate again, and he lost again.

At 51, he was elected the sixteenth President of the United States.

His name: Abraham Lincoln.

The marks of greatness are not suddenly delivered to us without failures, hardships, disappointments, loneliness, and loss. If we were to pick one man of the Bible whose life would fit this story, that man would be Joseph. Looking at Joseph's life toward the end, when Joseph was next to the ruler of Egypt himself, we can ask, How does he come to be next in power to Pharaoh?

This lesson will be presented in a mosaic. We will see the entire story of Joseph unfold, and we will see the great providential care of God in a way that is marvelous and inspiring.

ISRAEL AND EGYPT (37—50)

We now come to one of the central purposes of Genesis. It is easy to get Genesis confused. It is easy to think that Genesis was written for a group of reasons that had nothing to do with why the book was written. We said in the very beginning that it tells "the great story." This is a book about God and man. Chapters 37 through 50 have one central objective: to explain to the reader how Israel went into Egypt. When you begin Exodus, Israel is in Egypt. How in the world did Israel get there? Chapters 37 through 50 were written to show us.

Chapter 37 begins with Israel in Canaan. God is going to take Israel down to Egypt, and we see why. Israel is living in Canaan, which has little isolated tribes and city-states in it. They are being dug up today. Magazines carry articles about the household gods that are being dug up in Canaan. These idols are like the ones that Rachel put in the saddlebags when she left home. Samples of their language and some of their customs are being dug up. They did not worship the one true God of Abraham, Isaac, and Jacob. The people of Israel are slowly beginning to assimilate into the Canaanites. They are beginning to think like them. They are beginning to worship their gods.

What will the true and living God do? He is going to remove them from their homes and put them in Egypt where He can get their attention. Has that not happened to us? When our lives have been going in the wrong direction, He had to get our attention. Israel is losing their contact with God, so God decides to take them to Egypt. They go as a group of loose tribes, but they will come out forged as a great nation, loving and worshiping God and ultimately following God to Canaan.

JOSEPH AND EGYPT (37)

In 37:1-11, Joseph is introduced to us as a seventeen-year-old boy. He has two dreams which are duplicates of each other. As the great Egyptian historian Cyrus Gordon said, this is "typical of ancient Near East literature."[1] We will find during the rest of the book that there are many dreams, and they are in duplicate. There are two dreams: one by a baker and another by a cupbearer. Pharaoh has two dreams, and Joseph has duplicate dreams. His dreams simply point out, as his sheaf stands and everyone else in the family bows down to him, that he is superior to his mother, his father, and the rest of the family.

Jacob gives Joseph a robe. The robe represents the managerial position in the family. This is not simply a Christmas gift. The robe means that Joseph is the manager of his brothers. Judah, Simeon, and Reuben are all older brothers, and they immediately see the preferential treatment going to this younger brother. He has been given the robe of management, and along with that goes privilege. The brothers become jealous. In 37:12-36, they decide to sell him into slavery to the Midianites. That is the last they will see of him for

---

[1]Cyrus Gordon, *Ancient Near East* (New York: W. W. Norton & Co., 1965), 134.

many, many years. Do not overlook the fact that the Midianites are headed for Egypt.

Now we get to one of the most fascinating things about Genesis—this international picture of nations. Egypt is well to the south of Israel, but notice the contacts between them. Contacts between these ancient nations sometimes took place by military invasion, trade, intermarriage, travel, and in this instance, slavery. Joseph is a worshiper of Yahweh. He apparently speaks some form of Hebrew language. He is seventeen years old and looks and thinks like a Hebrew. He can say that Isaac and Jacob are his grandfather and his father, but now he is in Egypt facing a different religion, a different language, a different food, a different philosophy, a different culture—a totally different place.

AN INTERRUPTION (38)

The story of Joseph is now interrupted, and we have a story within a story. Why? One reason is suspense. Joseph is now down in Egypt, but we will not read any more about Egypt for a chapter. Instead, we will read of the family history of Israel. This is the story of Judah who has three children. Er is the first one who marries and shortly dies. Tamar, his widow, is to then be married to one of the other sons of Judah, but Judah prevents it. She then, seeing what has happened, traps Judah, her father-in-law, into adultery with her and calls for his ring and his staff. He leaves them with her, but more importantly, he has prevented what is called *levirate* responsibility. "Levirate" is built on the Latin word *levir* meaning "brother." In the ancient times of Israel, if a man dies and leaves his wife childless, his brother is to then marry her and have a child by her to continue the family history. Judah prevents that from happening with his other son. He is trapped into sex with her due to his own weakness. Judah says when she confronts him with the evidence, "She is more righteous than I." The lesson is clear to the Israelites: "Fulfill your levirate responsibility no matter how high the cost. If the great Judah could not get away with it, you will not either."

JOSEPH AND POTIPHAR (39)

Joseph becomes the official to Potiphar, the captain of the guard of Egypt. Potiphar's wife tries to trap Joseph into fornication. When Joseph runs from her, his coat is left behind. She screams to her husband and accuses Joseph of trying to rape her. Potiphar becomes angry, and he sends Joseph to the prison dungeon of Egypt. The last verse in this chapter reads,

> . . . the Lord was with him; and whatever he did, the Lord made to prosper (39:23).

JOSEPH AND PRISON (40)

Joseph is now in prison, and we read again of duplicate dreams. The cupbearer sees the dream of three branches of grapes. He squeezes the grapes into the cup and gives it to Pharaoh in the dream. Pharaoh drinks the cup. Joseph says that only God can interpret dreams. What the dream means is this: "The three branches mean three days, and in three days you will be restored to your position as cupbearer, the most trusted position in all of Egypt." The baker comes and says, "I have dreamed that there were three baskets, and the ravens came and ate out of them." Joseph must have shaken his head because he had to tell the baker, "That means in three days the birds will come and eat your flesh as they ate the bread from the baskets in your dream, and you will be killed by Pharaoh." The dreams come true. Joseph had asked the cupbearer to remember when he became restored to his position that he was still in the dungeon in Egypt, but the cupbearer does not remember.

JOSEPH AND PHARAOH (41)

Only when Pharaoh begins to have dreams is Joseph remembered by the cupbearer. Pharaoh sends for Joseph and meets Joseph for the first time.

> Then Pharaoh sent and called for Joseph, and they hurriedly brought him out of the dungeon; and when he had shaved himself and changed his clothes, he came to Pharaoh (41:14).

Hebrews do not shave their heads; Egyptians do. In order to look like an Egyptian, Joseph dresses appropriately before Pharaoh. When Joseph leaves the dungeon, he shaves his head, bathes, puts on the appropriate Egyptian clothing, and goes in to meet the greatest leader in the Mediterranean world, Pharaoh. Pharaoh tells of the great story of the seven lean cows in his dream who come up out of the River Nile and eat the seven fat cows, but no magician or wise man in all of Egypt knows the meaning of this. Joseph says the interpretation of dreams belongs to God and tells him, "I am God's man, and I want to tell you what that means. There will be seven years of great growth and plenty in the land of Egypt, followed by seven years of famine. Clearly, it is in the best interest of Egypt, therefore, that during the seven years of plenty there be storehouses of food established for the seven years of famine." God shows Pharaoh, through Joseph, the true meaning of the dream.

> "And now let Pharaoh look for a man discerning and wise, and set him over the land of Egypt" (41:33).

It is at this point that Pharaoh chooses Joseph. This places Joseph over the entire land of Egypt.

So Pharaoh said to Joseph, "Since God has in-
formed you of all this, there is no one so discerning
and wise as you are. You shall be over my house,
and according to your command all my people
shall do homage; only in the throne I will be
greater than you" (41:39, 40).

Pharaoh is beginning to use God-language, the language of a Jew, of a Hebrew, as he brings before Joseph
the opportunity to rule the land. It is not clear from the
text if Pharaoh had previous knowledge of God, but he
now begins to discuss God as the source of wisdom for
Joseph.

JOSEPH AND THE FAMINE (42—44)

As a famine develops north of Egypt, there is the
opportunity for the family of Joseph and his brothers to
move down and to borrow or buy food from the great
breadbasket of the ancient world. The brothers begin to
visit Egypt, but they do not recognize Joseph. He is
shaven and speaks the language of the Egyptian. He
was seventeen the last time they saw him. Now he is the
ruler of Egypt, second only to Pharaoh. He reads Egyptian cuneiform. He knows the wise men of Egypt, the
philosophy, the music, the people, and how to think as
an Egyptian. Suddenly, here are his brothers whom he
recognizes, but they do not recognize him, asking to do
business. Remember, the last time he saw them, they
sold him into slavery.

In order to test them, he accuses them of espionage.
He attacks their motivation by asserting that they
want to overthrow Egypt. They convince him there is a
famine in the north, that their old father has sent them
down to Egypt because they are hungry. In 42:18-38,
Joseph begins to supply their needs.

In chapter 44, there is the wonderful story of the
silver cup of Joseph which he orders the steward to put
into the sack of the youngest. They retrieve it, and there

is the severe test in which Judah steps forward and says Benjamin cannot be kept in Egypt. It will break his father's heart. Judah reasons that his father only had two sons whom he really loved; one of them is dead and gone (of course, he is speaking of Joseph), and the other is this son whose name is Benjamin. Judah gave his word that Benjamin would return. Joseph is touched in his heart as he sees what has occurred to Judah, the oldest of his brothers, and the way in which his heart has mellowed and changed over the years.

JOSEPH AND HIS BROTHERS (45—49)

Chapter 45 tells of the great scene in Egypt.

> Then Joseph could not control himself before all those who stood by him, and he cried, "Have everyone go out from me." So there was no man with him when Joseph made himself known to his brothers. And he wept so loudly that the Egyptians heard it, and the household of Pharaoh heard of it. Then Joseph said to his brothers, "I am Joseph! Is my father still alive?" But his brothers could not answer him, for they were dismayed at his presence. Then Joseph said to his brothers, "Please come closer to me." And they came closer. And he said, "I am your brother Joseph, whom you sold into Egypt. And now do not be grieved or angry with yourselves, because you sold me here; for God sent me before you to preserve life. For the famine has been in the land these two years, and there are still five years in which there will be neither plowing nor harvesting. And God sent me before you to preserve for you a remnant in the earth, and to keep you alive by a great deliverance" (45:1-7).

He continues to show this incredible trust in the providence of God. It is God who has been doing this. It is God who has brought his brothers to Egypt. It is God who has done this to save their family from hunger and from dying in Canaan.

In chapter 46, Joseph sends for Jacob and all of the

family who move to Egypt. They settle in the land of Goshen where they become shepherds for the rest of Jacob's life.

In chapter 47, there is a great moment when Jacob himself blesses Pharaoh.

> Then Joseph brought his father Jacob and presented him to Pharaoh; and Jacob blessed Pharaoh. And Pharaoh said to Jacob, "How many years have you lived?" So Jacob said to Pharaoh, "The years of my sojourning are one hundred and thirty; few and unpleasant have been the years of my life, nor have they attained the years that my fathers lived during the days of their sojourning." And Jacob blessed Pharaoh, and went out from his presence. So Joseph settled his father and his brothers, and gave them a possession in the land of Egypt, in the best of the land, in the land of Rameses, as Pharaoh had ordered. And Joseph provided his father and his brothers and all his father's household with food, according to their little ones (47:7-12).

Cyrus Gordon says Genesis is the key document in the world for understanding this period of Egyptian history. The Word of God was not written in a vacuum. Genesis is a great document showing us the validity of the Word of God. It squares with history.

In chapters 48 and 49, Joseph, along with his brothers, goes before Jacob. Jacob blesses his sons.

> All these are the twelve tribes of Israel, and this is what their father said to them when he blessed them. He blessed them, every one with the blessing appropriate to him (49:28).

Then Jacob dies.

JOSEPH AND JACOB (50)

> Then Joseph fell on his father's face, and wept over him and kissed him (50:1).

Joseph had spent most of his life away from his

father. He did not even know if his dad was living. He had seventeen years with his father, and at the very end of his life he had time with him. But, most of his life, Joseph did not even know if Jacob was living. But he loved him, and when Jacob died, he threw himself on the body of Jacob and wept loudly.

Joseph was able to cry. He was able to show his emotions and his feelings. Here is a real man, and twice in these last few chapters of Genesis, he wept and cried so loudly that even the household of Pharaoh could hear him. He is a great man of feeling and emotion.

In the latter part of this chapter, we read of Joseph's death. Notice that unlike the Hebrew burial, he is buried as an Egyptian, which means that he is embalmed.

> So Joseph died at the age of one hundred and ten years; and he was embalmed and placed in a coffin in Egypt (50:26).

What does the story of Joseph teach us?

First, people disappoint us. Everybody disappointed Joseph including his older brothers, the cupbearer, Potiphar, and others. People disappoint. You cannot put your ultimate hope in people.

Second, greatness is always forged in the furnace of disappointment. The great man, Joseph, faced many failures and problems. He was accused of adultery and fornication. No one around him understood him. Greatness is always forged in the furnace of failures, problems, and disappointments. Some of the greatest people we know are people who have gone through unemployment, illness, difficulty, and family hardships like Joseph.

Third, love is stronger than hate. The brothers of Joseph hated him. He loved them, and he won the great battle. In any given moment, violence and hatred may seem to win, but love always surfaces as the final winner. No wonder so much Scripture encourages us to love each other, because love is stronger than hate.

Fourth, you are greater than your circumstances. Joseph could have asked, "Why am I in prison? What am I doing here? Don't I ever have an answered prayer anymore?" But he knew that God was greater than his circumstances. Daily circumstances may be basically the same for many people. The difference in people is in their attitude toward their situations. The wind is constant. The difference is in the set of your sails.

Fifth, God guides the events of life. He guided the events of Joseph's life, and that same God is in control today. Does He move in mysterious ways? Sometimes He must get us isolated to get our attention. Why did Joseph go down to Egypt? Why did he want to know the cupbearer? Why did he want to know Pharaoh? Why did he want to interpret his dreams? Why is Joseph placed in high position? Why does a famine take place in the north? Why does Jacob's family go to Egypt for bread? The providence of God is a mystery. God is guiding the events in the lives of the great man Joseph.

CONCLUSION

"The great story" is the story of Genesis. The story begins with man and God in close relationship with each other. Sin and rebellion interrupt that relationship. But God, based on His own nature of mercy and love, provides for another way for the relationship to be re-established. He makes promises to man and asks for man to have faith in them. Those promises include the building of a great nation through whom the entire world will be blessed. Genesis ends where it begins. God and man are in close relationship, and God is about to build a great nation through whom Jesus will come.

QUESTIONS

1. What does God allow to happen to Joseph and other

people in this episode?

2. Select three of Joseph's brothers, and distinguish what qualities of character each demonstrates in the Joseph story.

3. Why did Jews love the Joseph story?

4. What does the story of Joseph teach us?

5. How does the Joseph story serve as a fitting conclusion to "the great story"?